THIS BOOK BELONGS TO

HIDDEN TREASURES

DISCOVER MORE
SCAN THE QR CODE

Embrace the Wealth Within

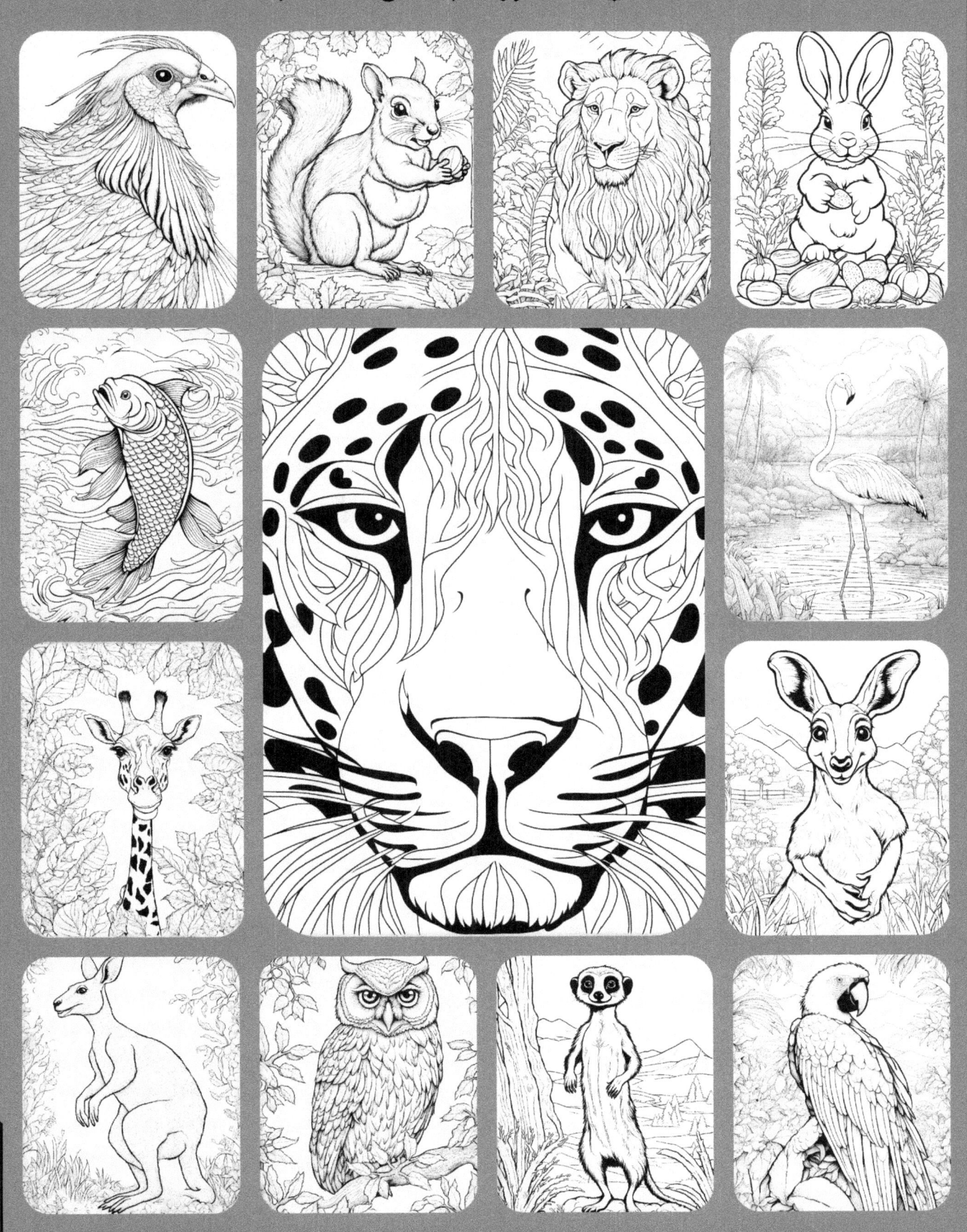

GREETINGS! ON A COLORFUL JOURNEY!

Welcome to the wonderful world of coloring! You have just purchased one of our amazing coloring books, and we are so happy to have you as part of our creative community.

Unwind and Unleash Creativity!

Coloring is not only fun, but also relaxing, therapeutic, and beneficial for your mental health. Whether you are looking for a way to unwind, express yourself, or simply enjoy some quality time with your favorite colors, you will find something to suit your mood and style in our coloring book.

Share Your Colorful Story!

We hope you enjoy every page of this book, and we would love to hear from you about your coloring experience. Please take a moment to leave a review on Amazon and share your thoughts and feedback with us and other colorists. Your opinion matters a lot to us and helps us improve our products and services.

Connect with Us!

If you have any questions, comments, or suggestions, please feel free to contact us at ooffoopub@gmail.com. We are always happy to hear from you and assist you in any way we can.

Explore Endless Creativity!

And don't forget to check out our other coloring book masterpieces! We have a variety of themes and styles for you to choose from, and we are constantly adding new books to our collection. You can find them all on our Amazon page or on our website.

Thank You for Choosing Colorful Adventures!

Thank you for choosing our coloring book, and happy coloring!

READ BEFORE START COLORING

Welcome to the Vibrant World of OOFFOO Coloring!

Dear Colorist,

Congratulations on choosing an OOFFOO coloring book! We're thrilled to have you embark on this artistic adventure with us. Before you dive into a world of color, we have a few tips to ensure your coloring experience is nothing short of amazing.

1. Gather Your Tools:
Before you begin, gather your coloring tools. Whether you prefer colored pencils, markers, or crayons, pick what suits your style. Test your colors on a separate sheet to ensure they're just right for the masterpiece you're about to create.

2. Create Your Oasis:
Set the stage for your coloring session. Play your favorite tunes, light a scented candle, or grab your go-to beverage. The more comfortable your space, the more magical your coloring journey will be.

3. Dare to Dream in Color:
This book is your canvas! Don't be afraid to color outside the lines and explore your creativity. Experiment with different color palettes and techniques—make each page uniquely yours.

4. Showcase Your Masterpiece:
We'd love to see your finished artwork! Share your creations on social media using #OOFFOOCreations and tag us @ooffoopublications. Your art could inspire fellow colorists around the globe.

5. Take Breaks, Embrace Relaxation:
Coloring is a therapeutic escape, so take breaks when needed. Step back, appreciate your work, and return with fresh eyes. Let the process be as enjoyable as the finished product.

6. Guard Your Pages:
Consider placing a sheet of paper between pages to prevent any color bleed-through, especially if you're using markers. This way, each page stays pristine and ready for display.

7. Enjoy Every Moment:
Above all, remember that coloring is meant to be joyful and relaxing. Lose yourself in the colors, leave your worries behind, and immerse yourself in the sheer pleasure of creating.

Thank you for choosing OOFFOO Publications. We hope our coloring book brings color and joy to your world. Happy coloring!

For inquiries, reach out to us at ooffoopub@gmail.com.

With artistic excitement,
OOFFOO Publications

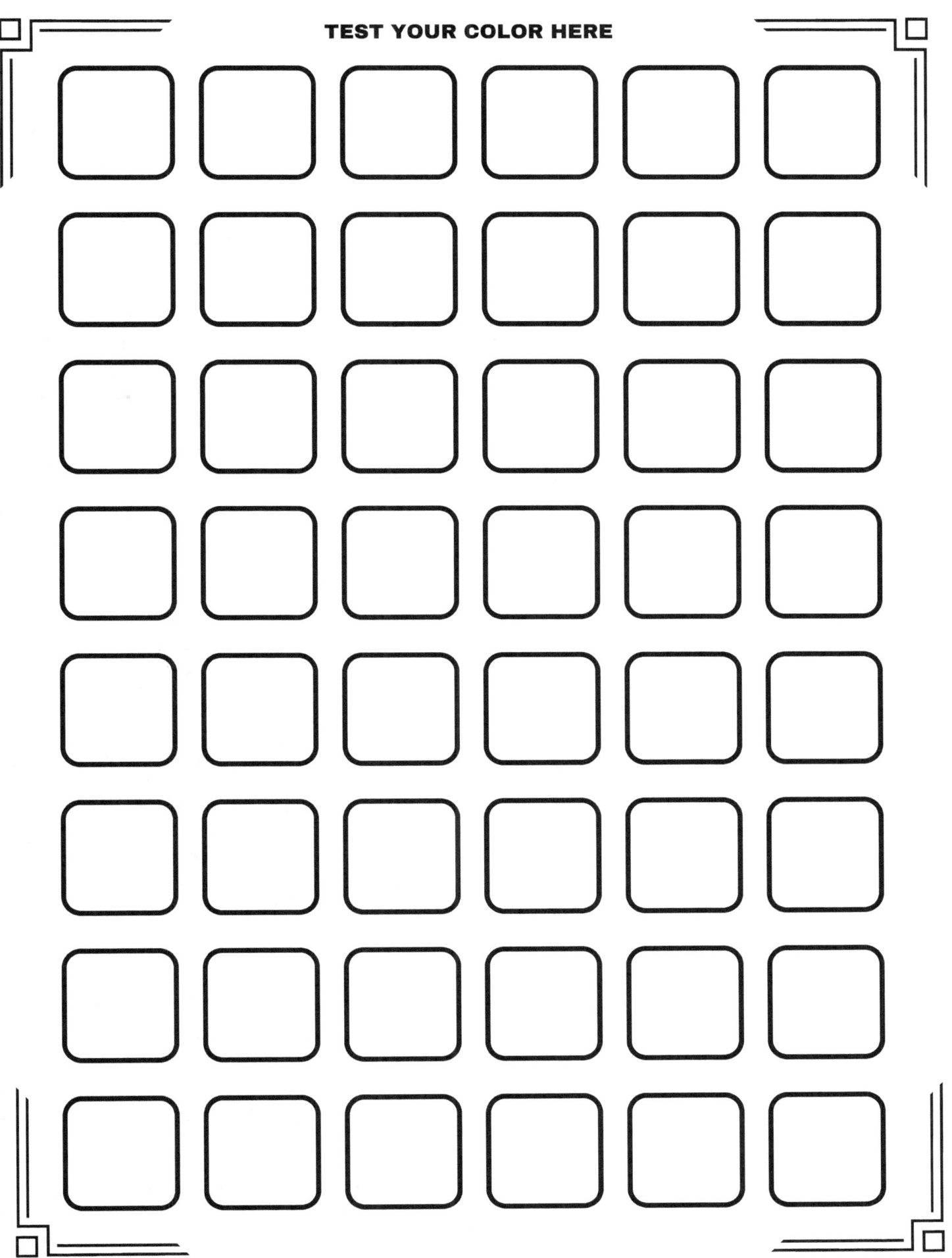

TEST YOUR COLOR HERE

TEST YOUR COLOR HERE

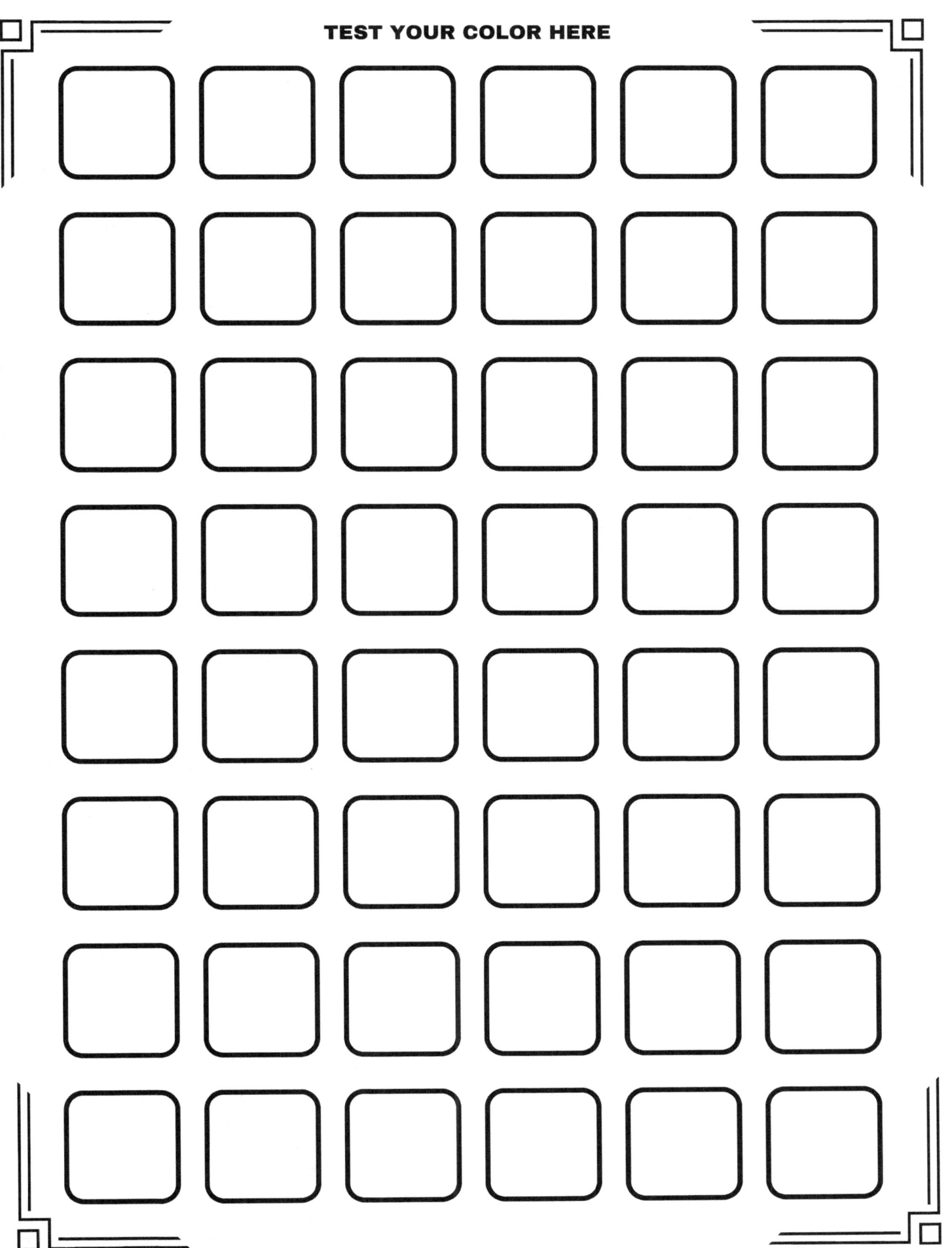

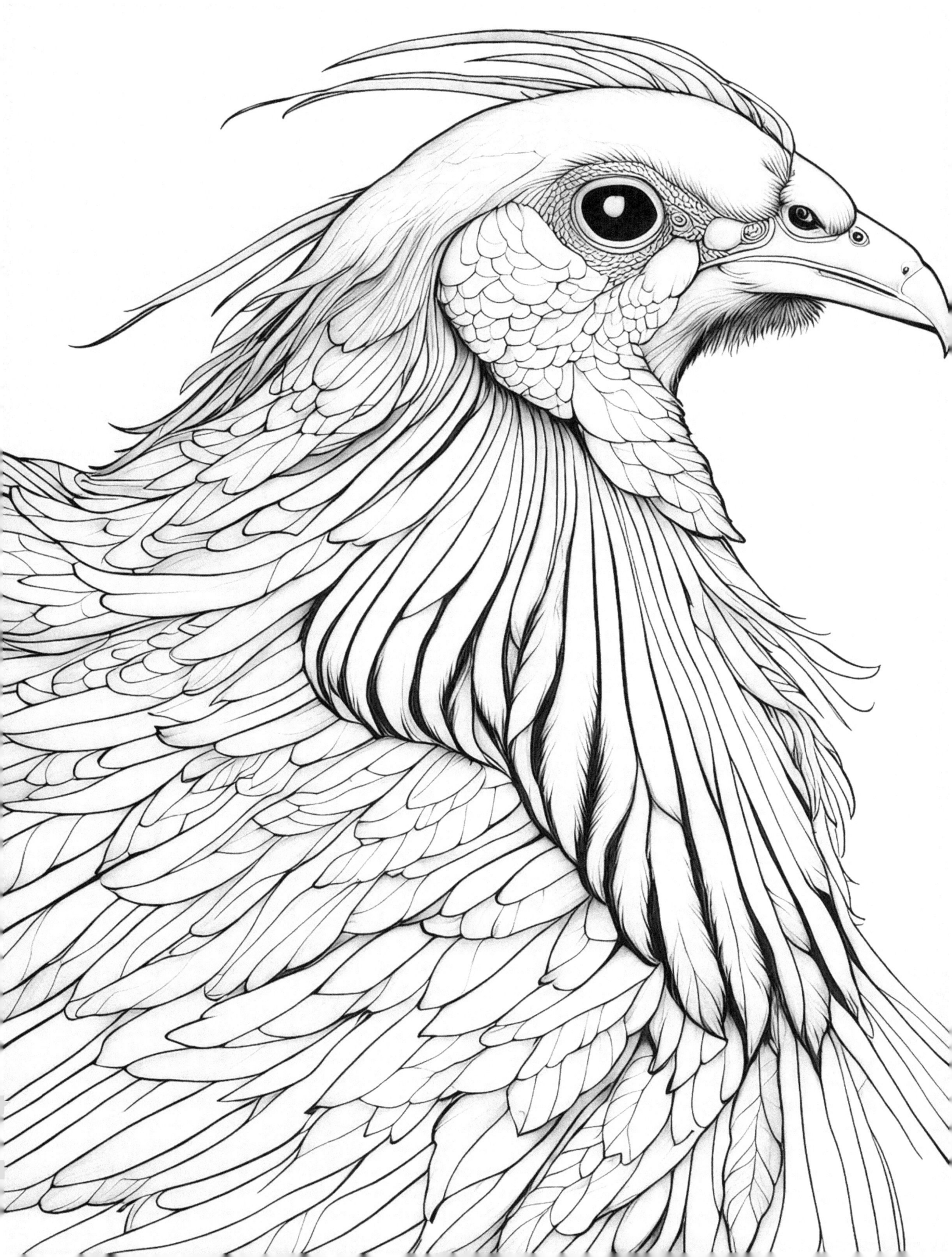

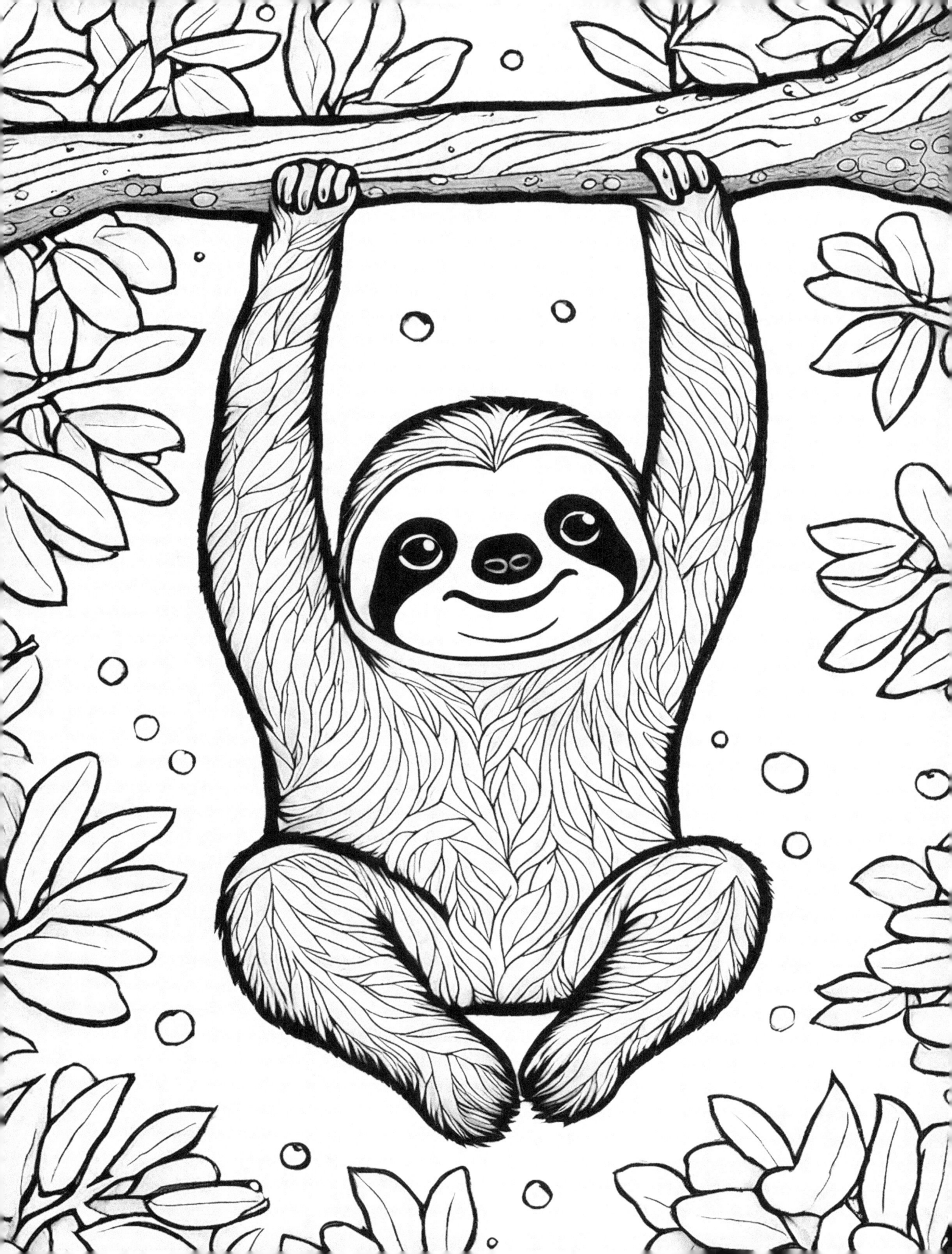

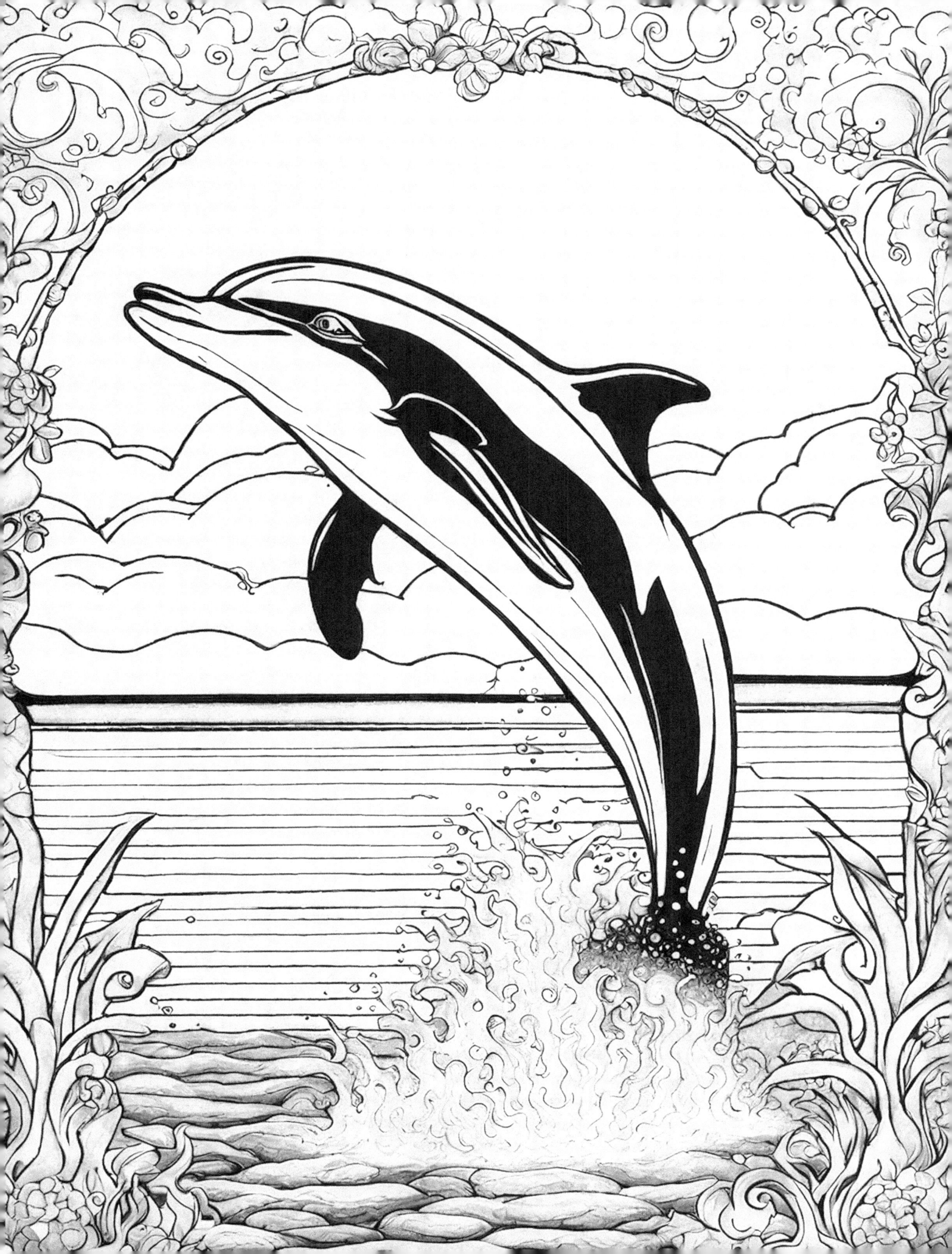

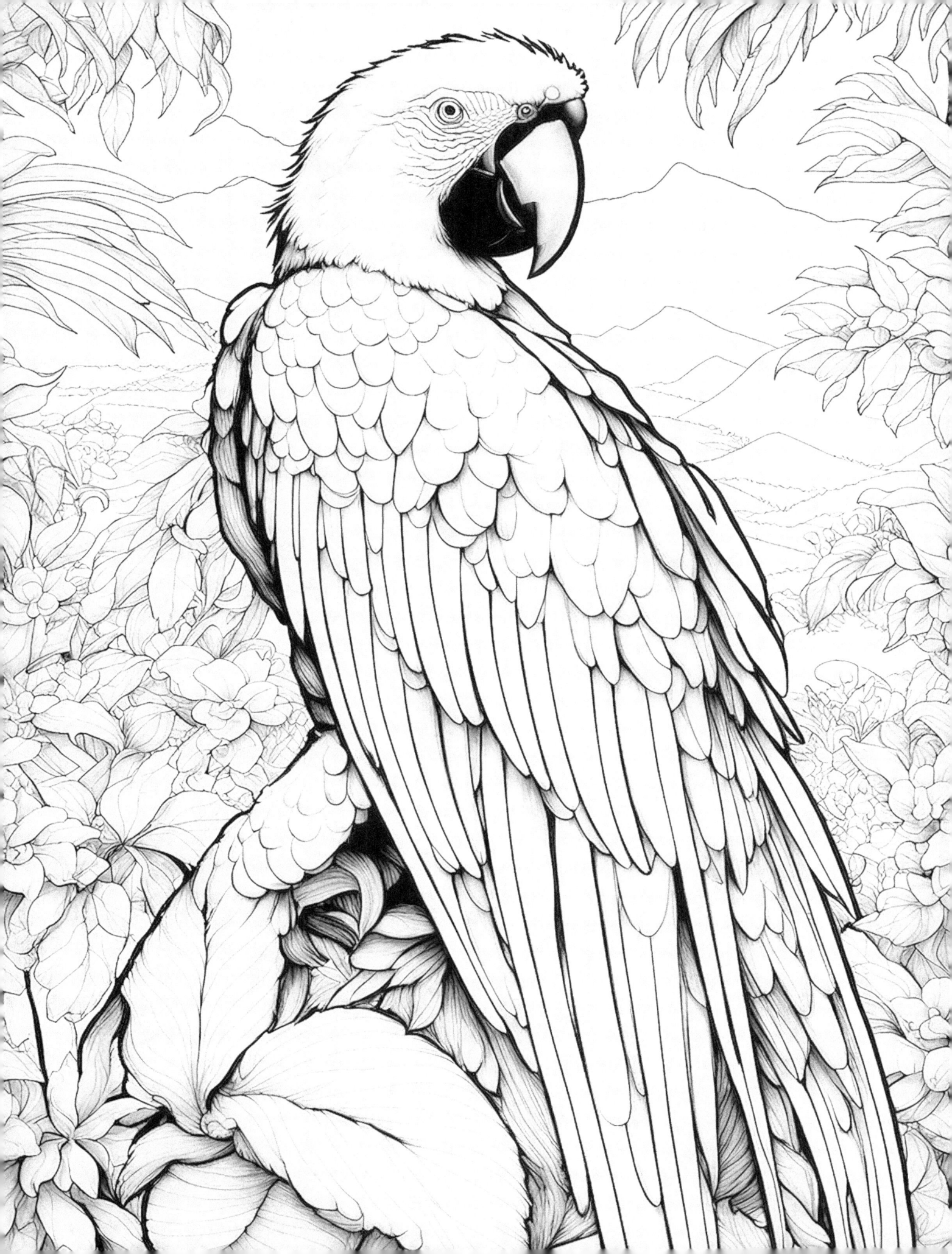

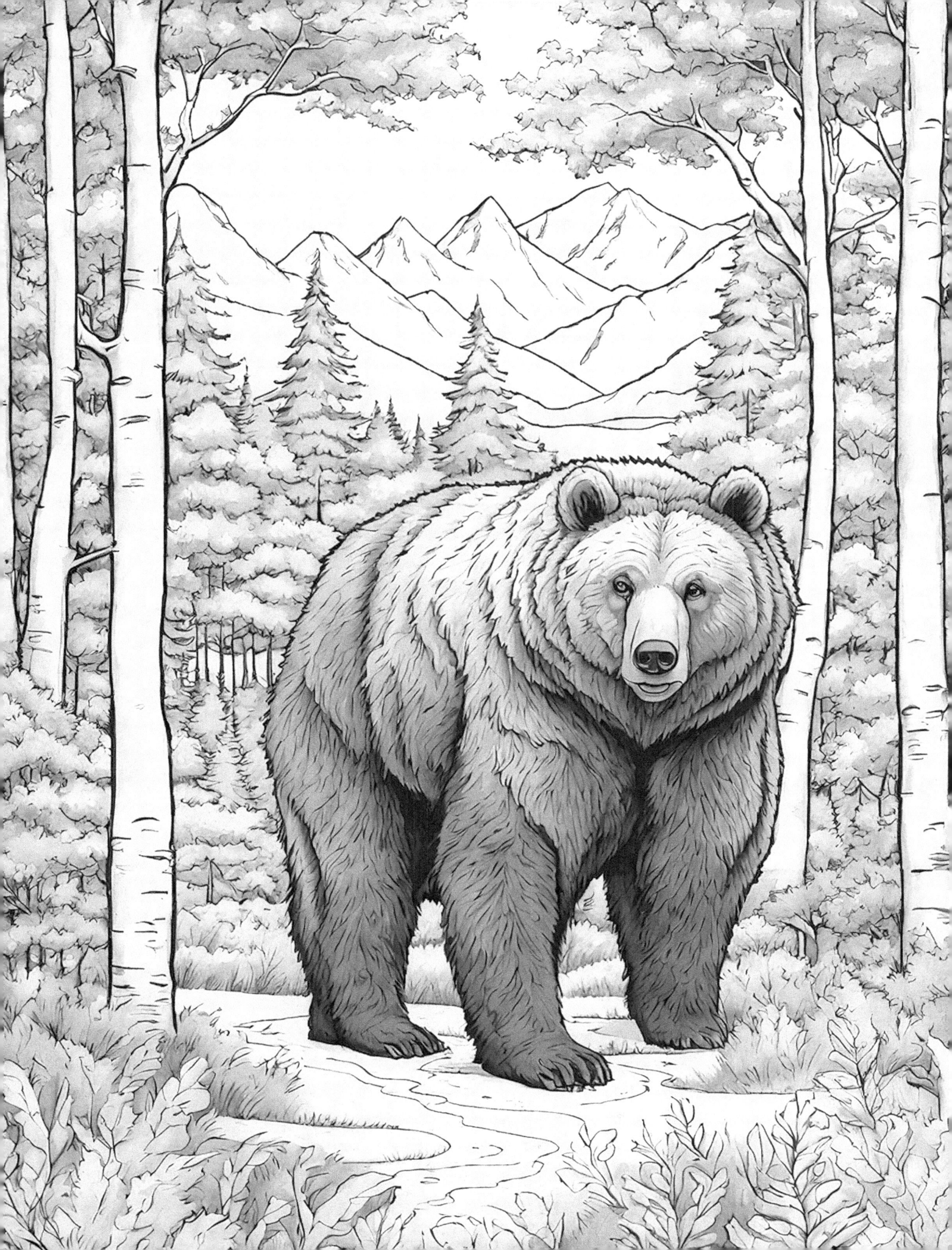

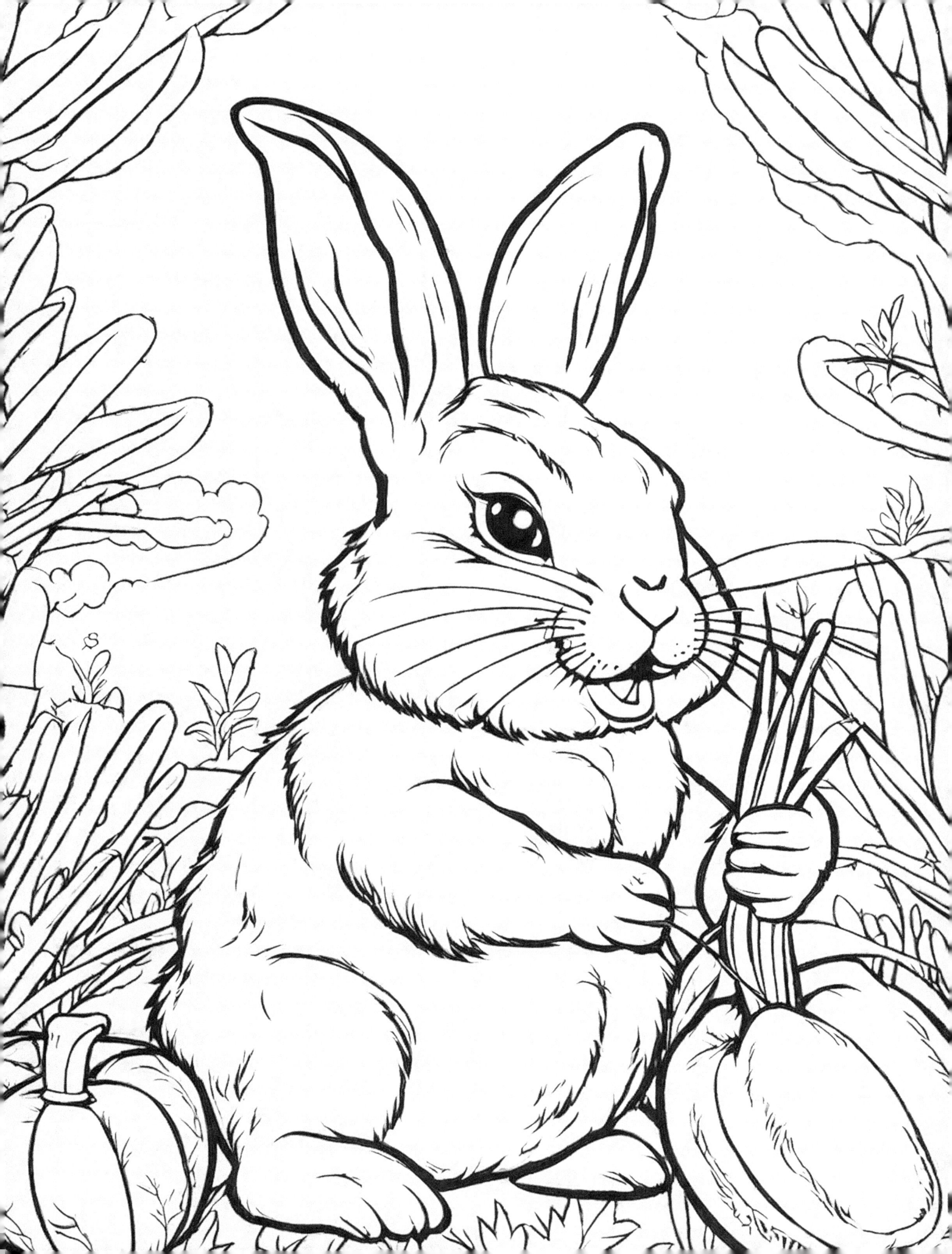

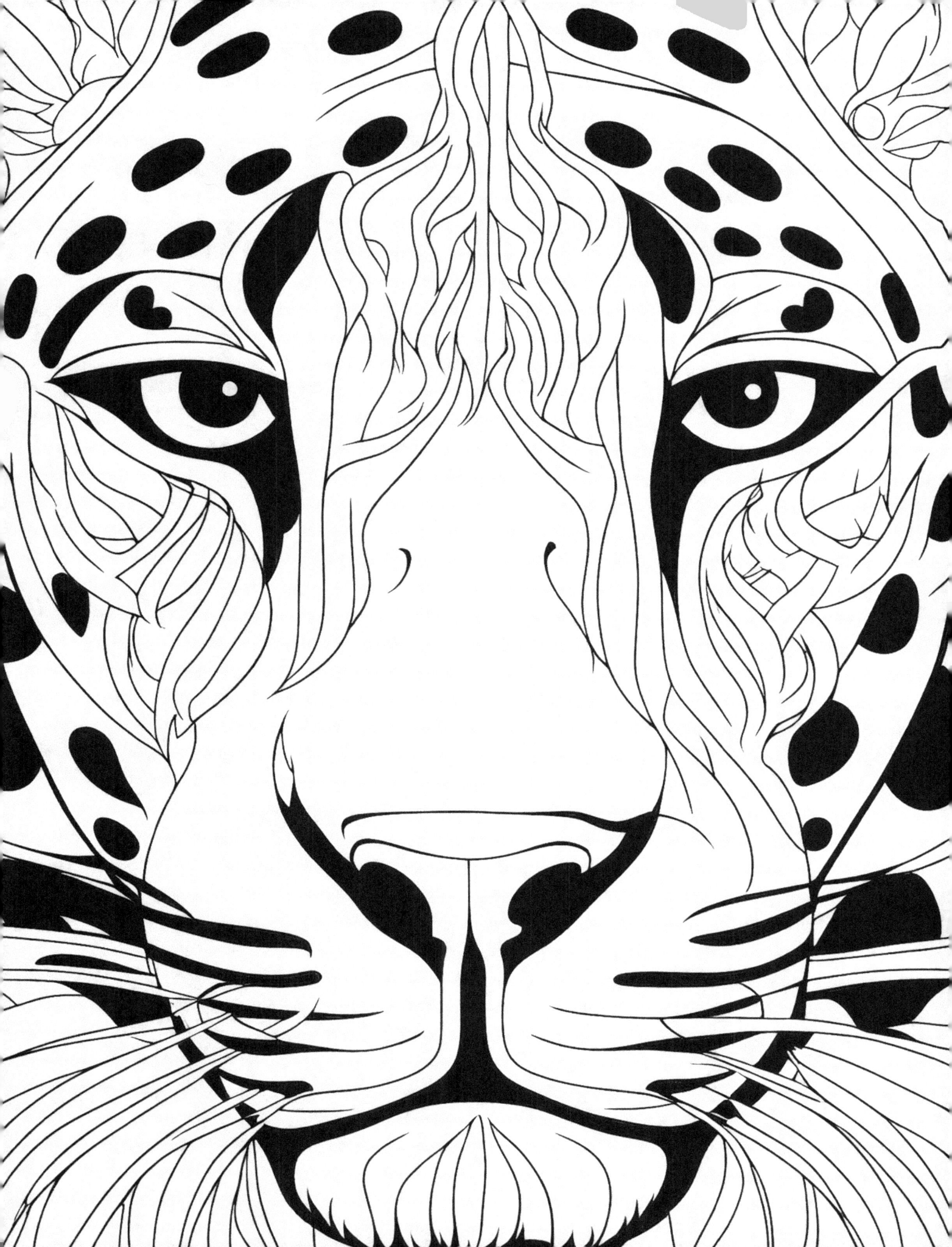

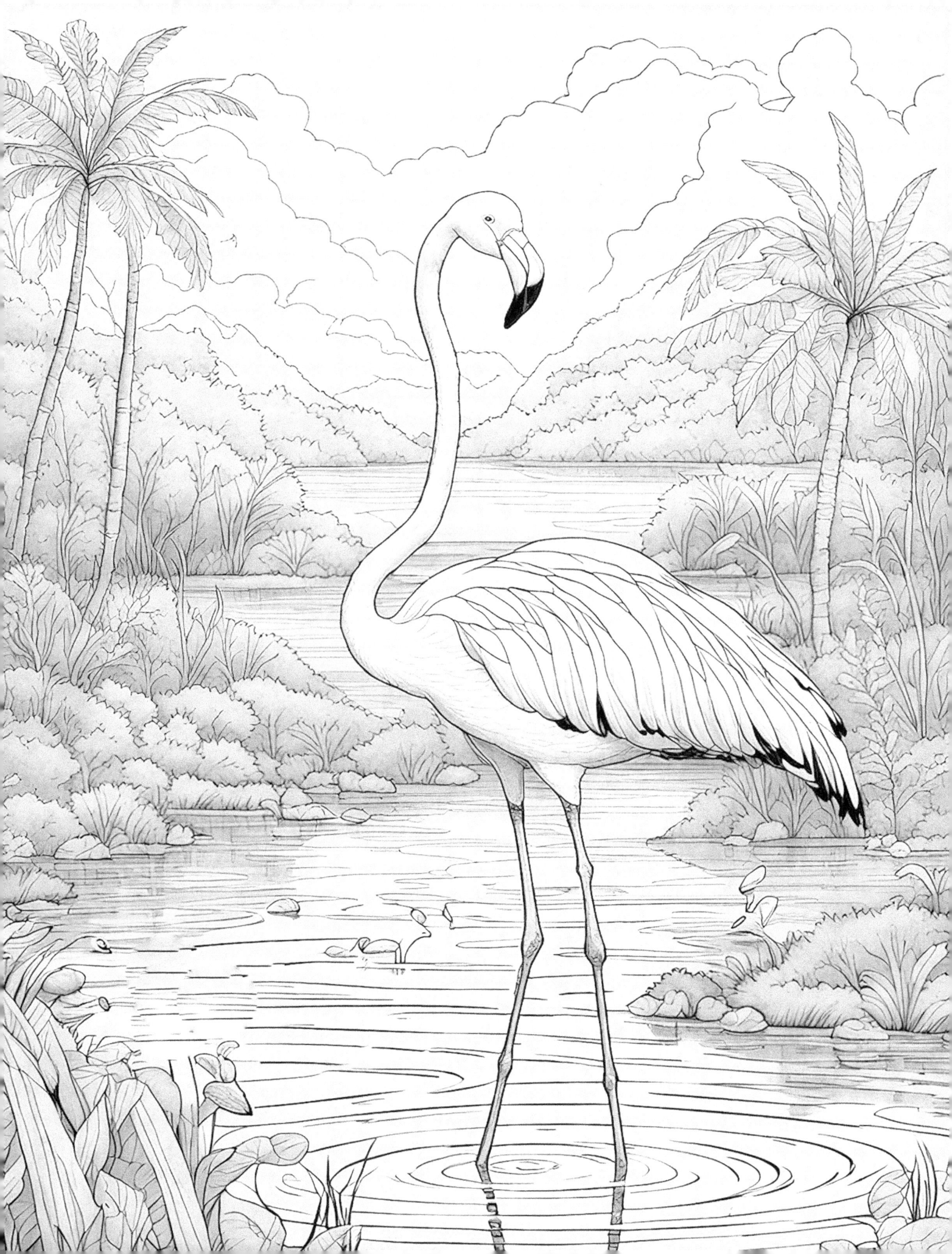

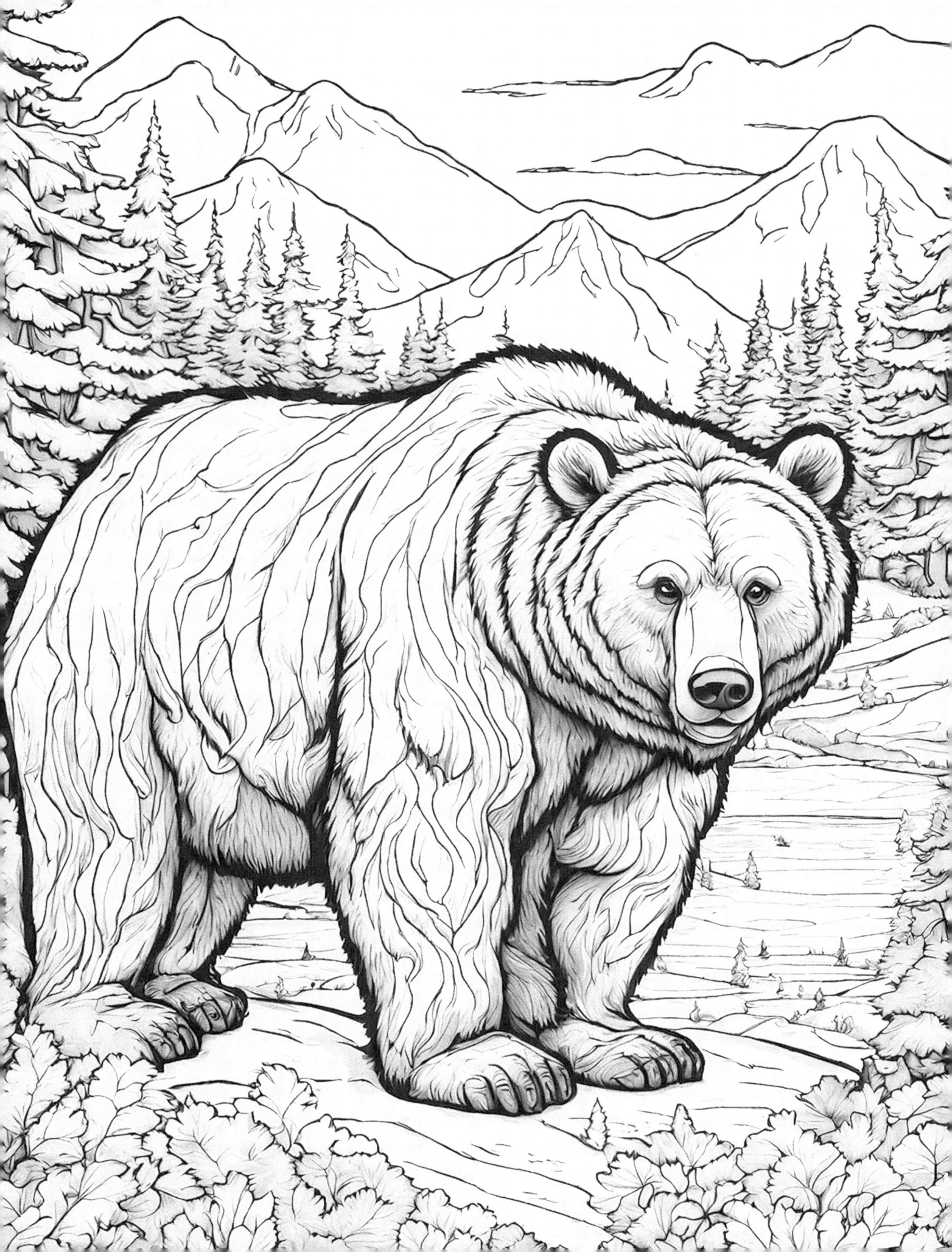

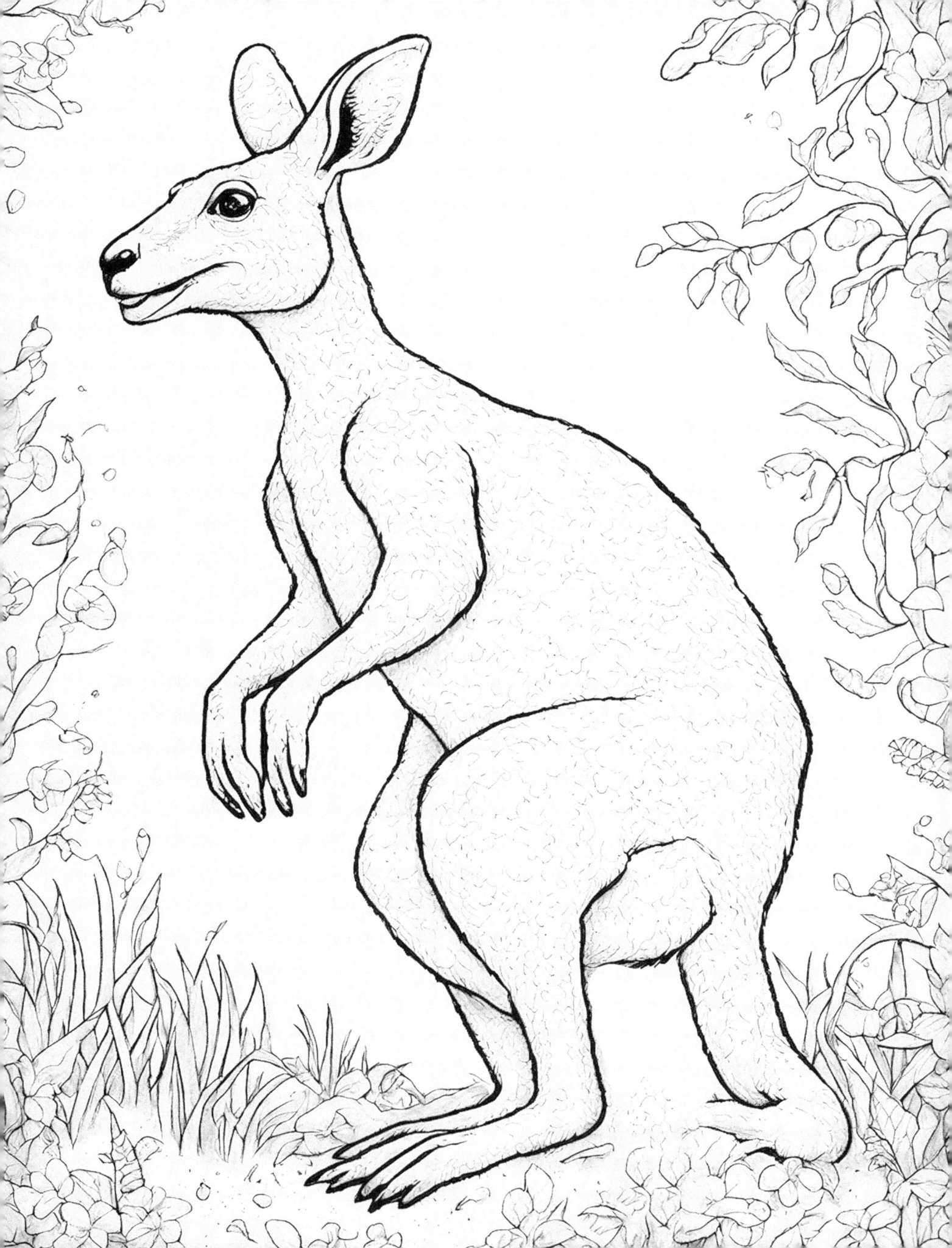

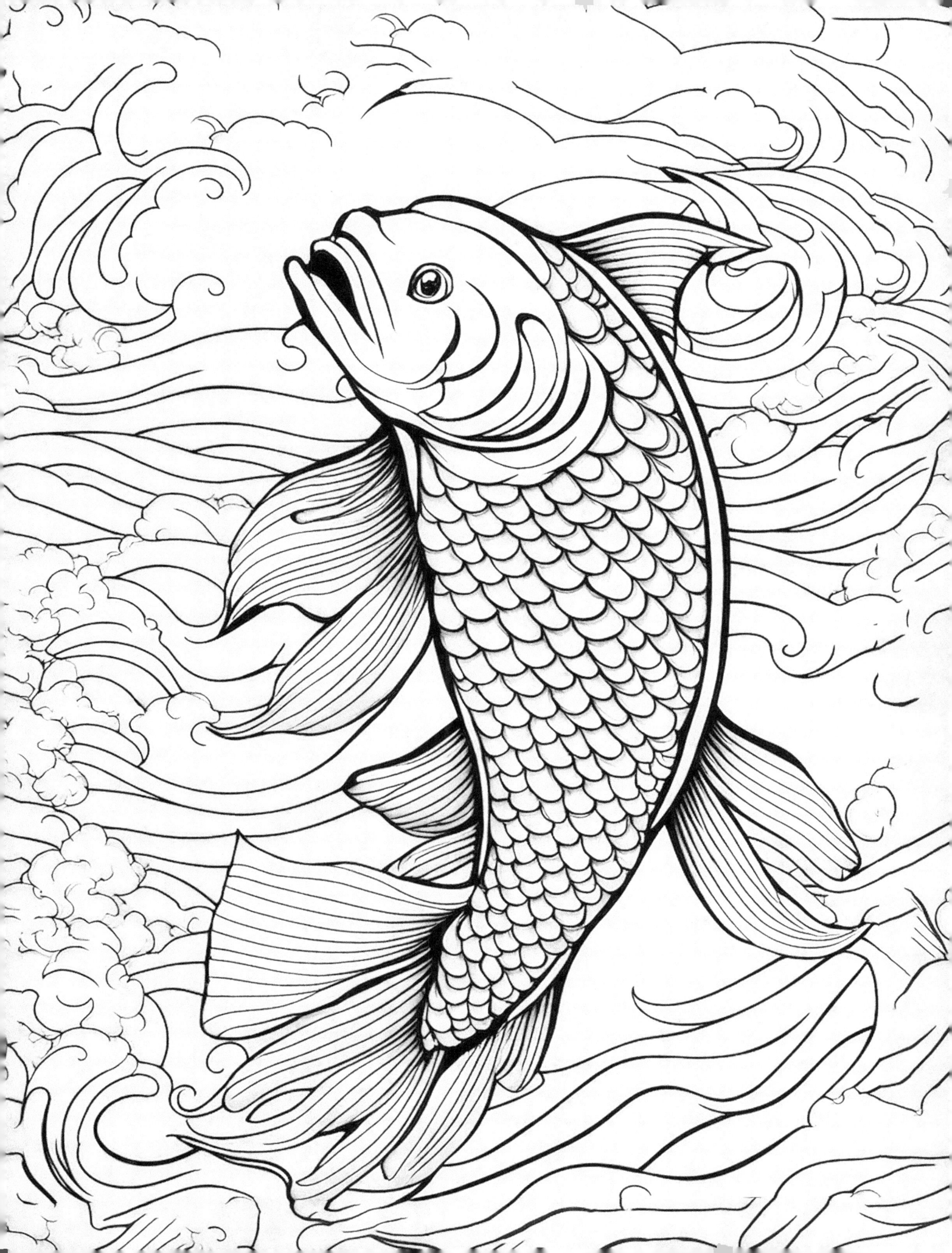

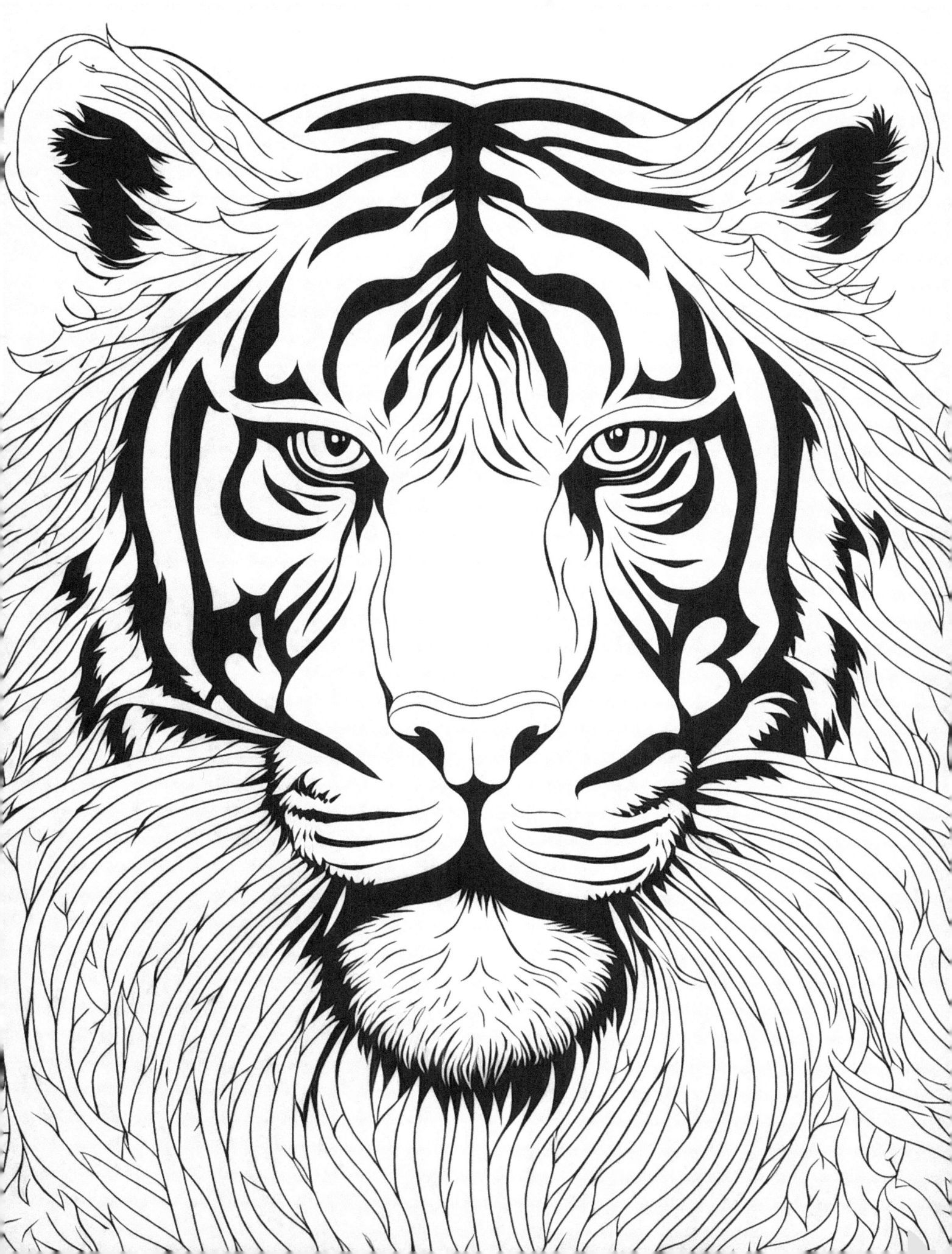

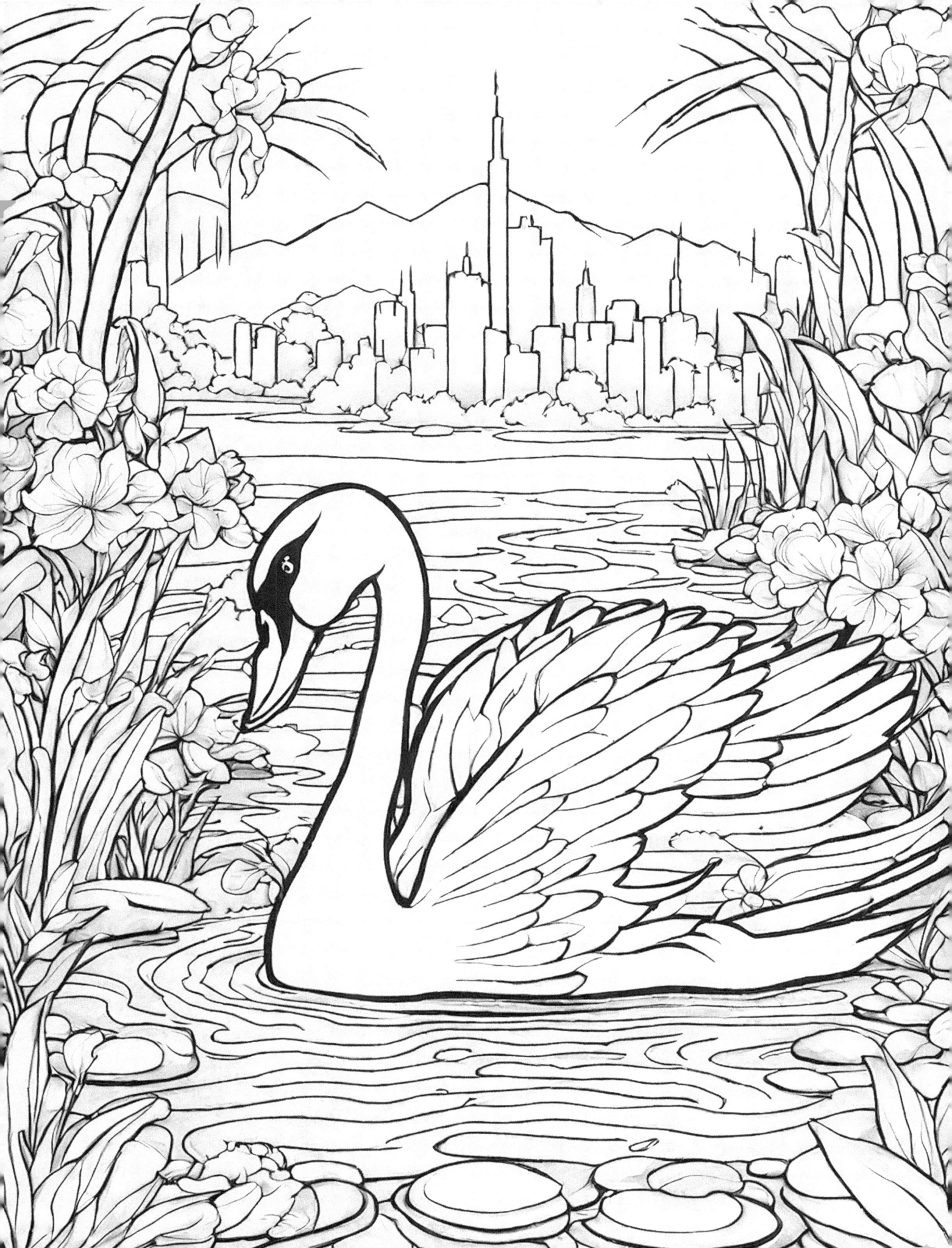

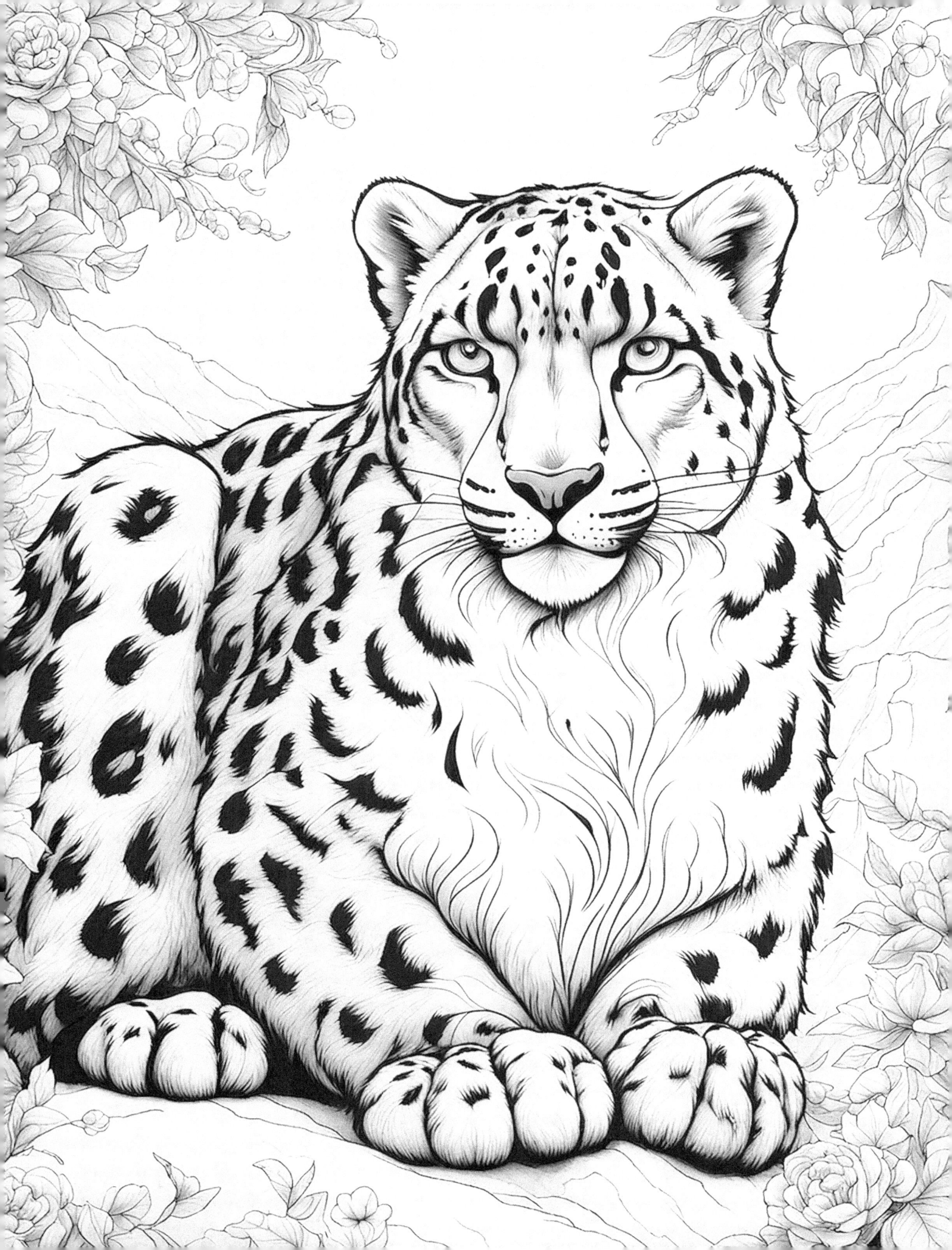

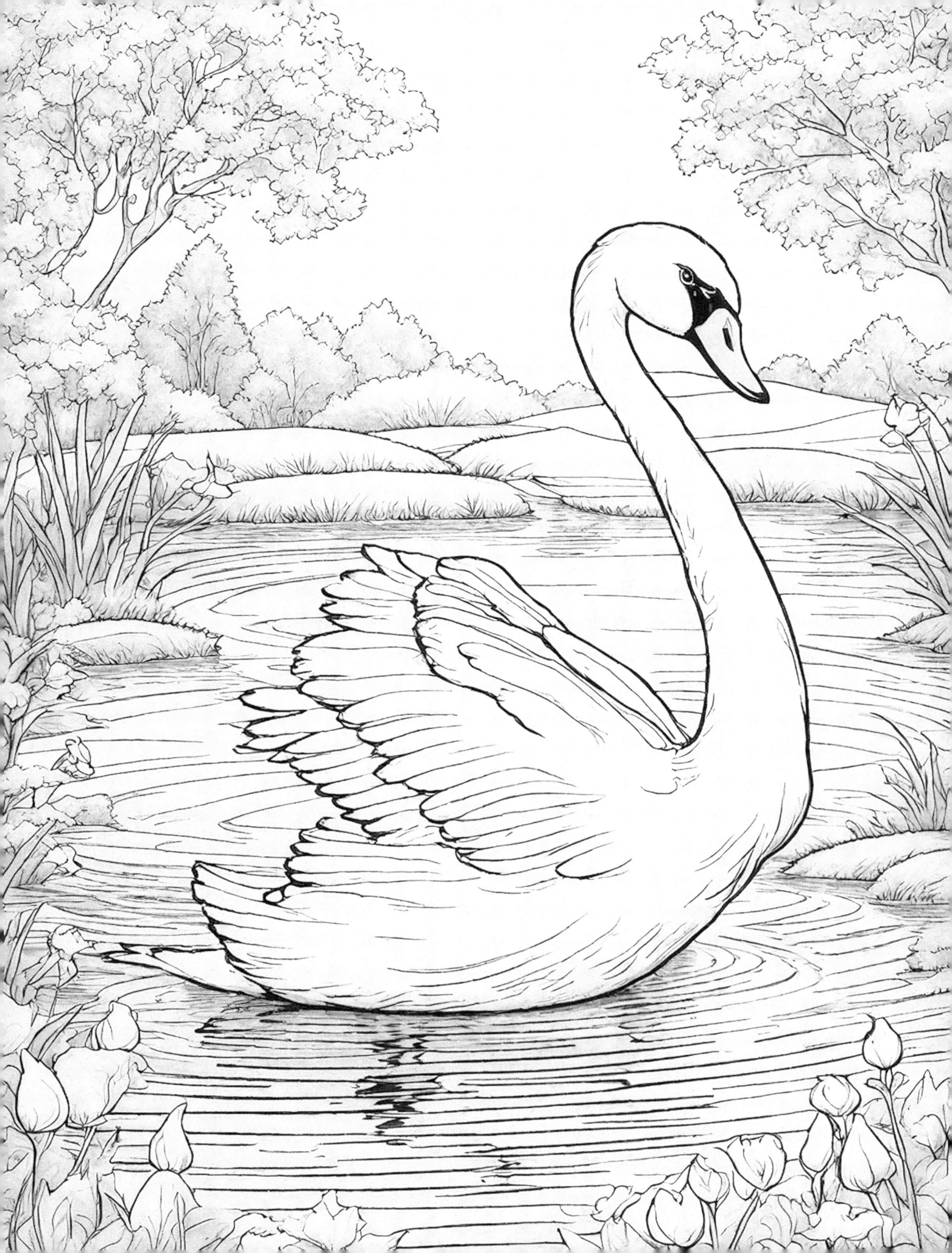

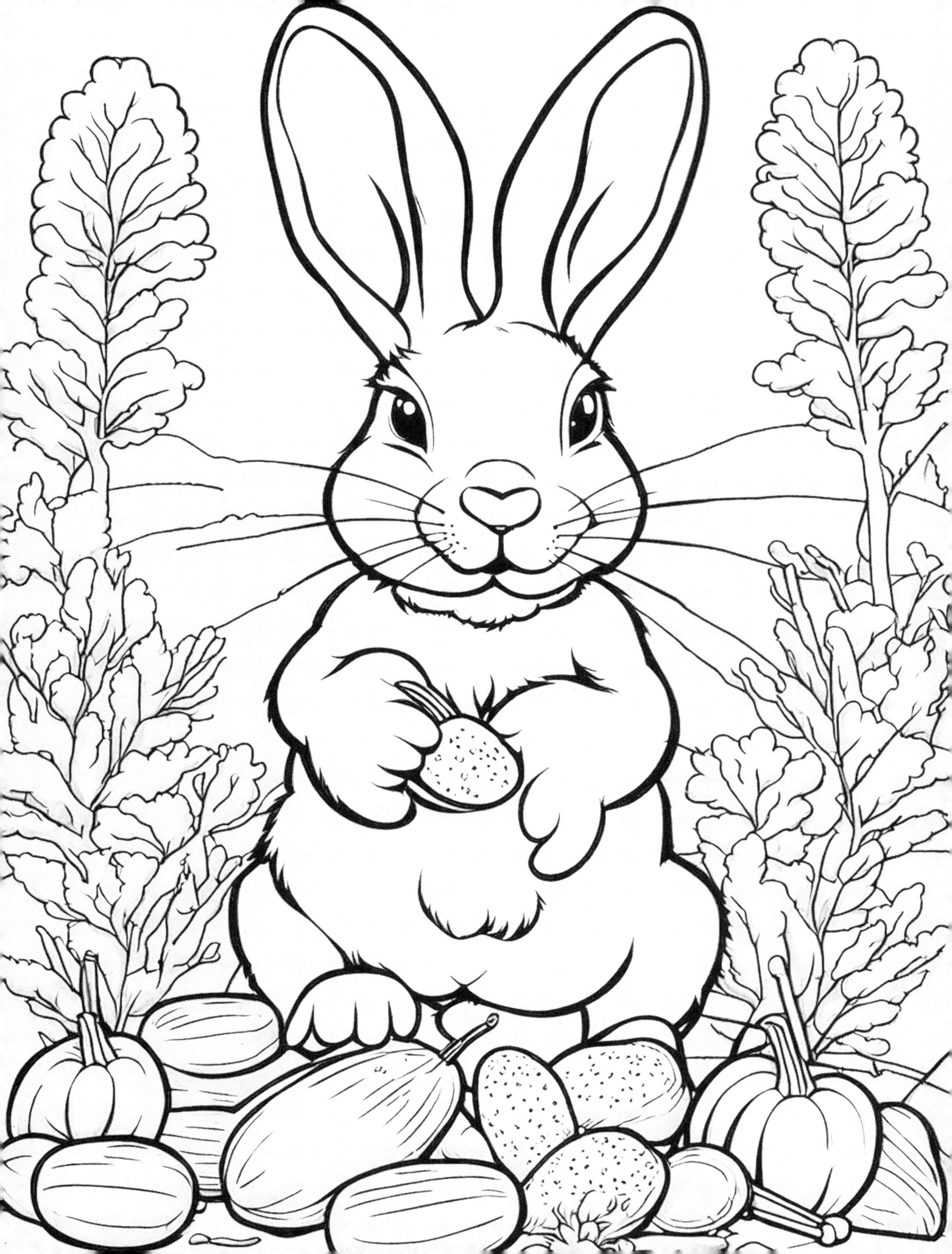

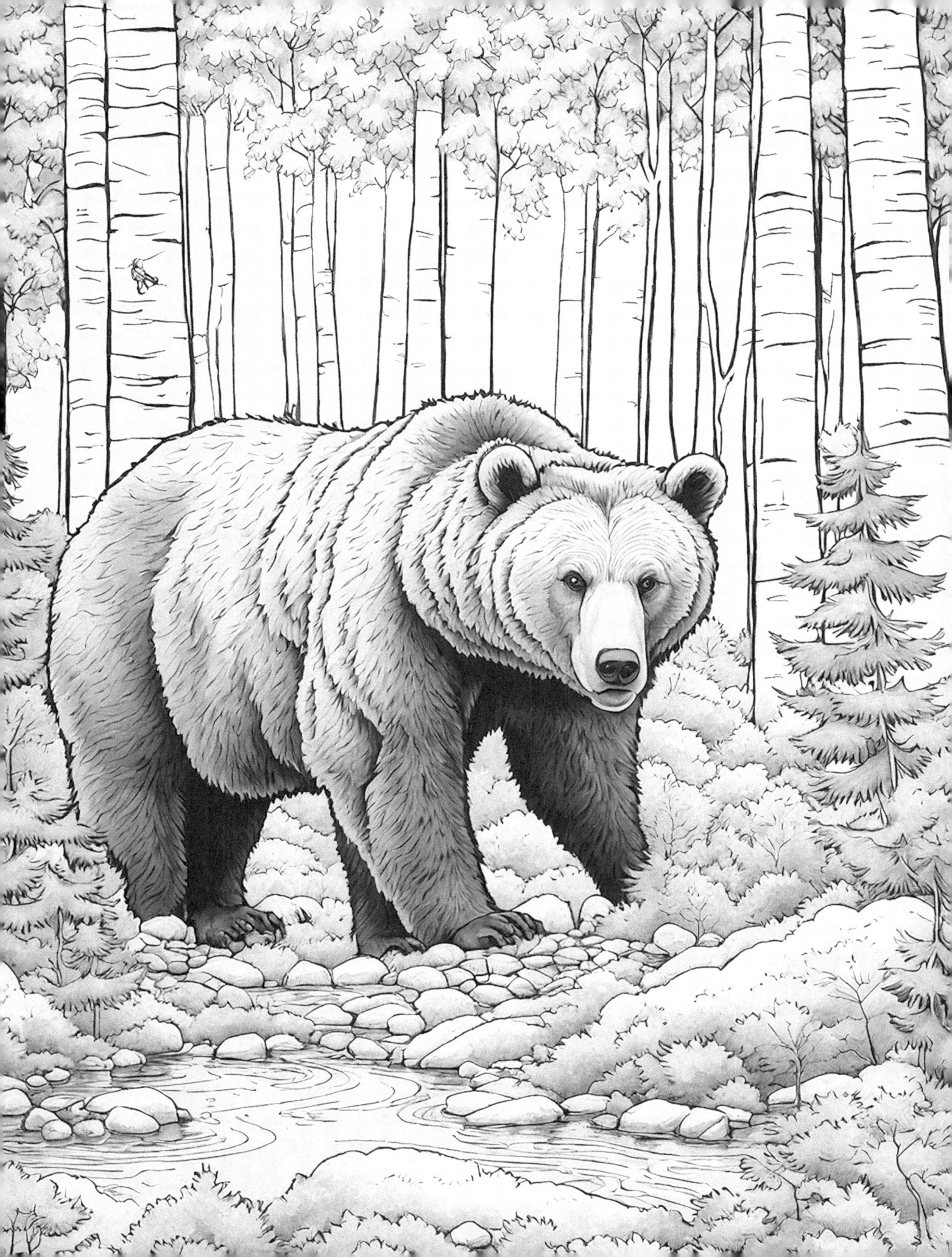

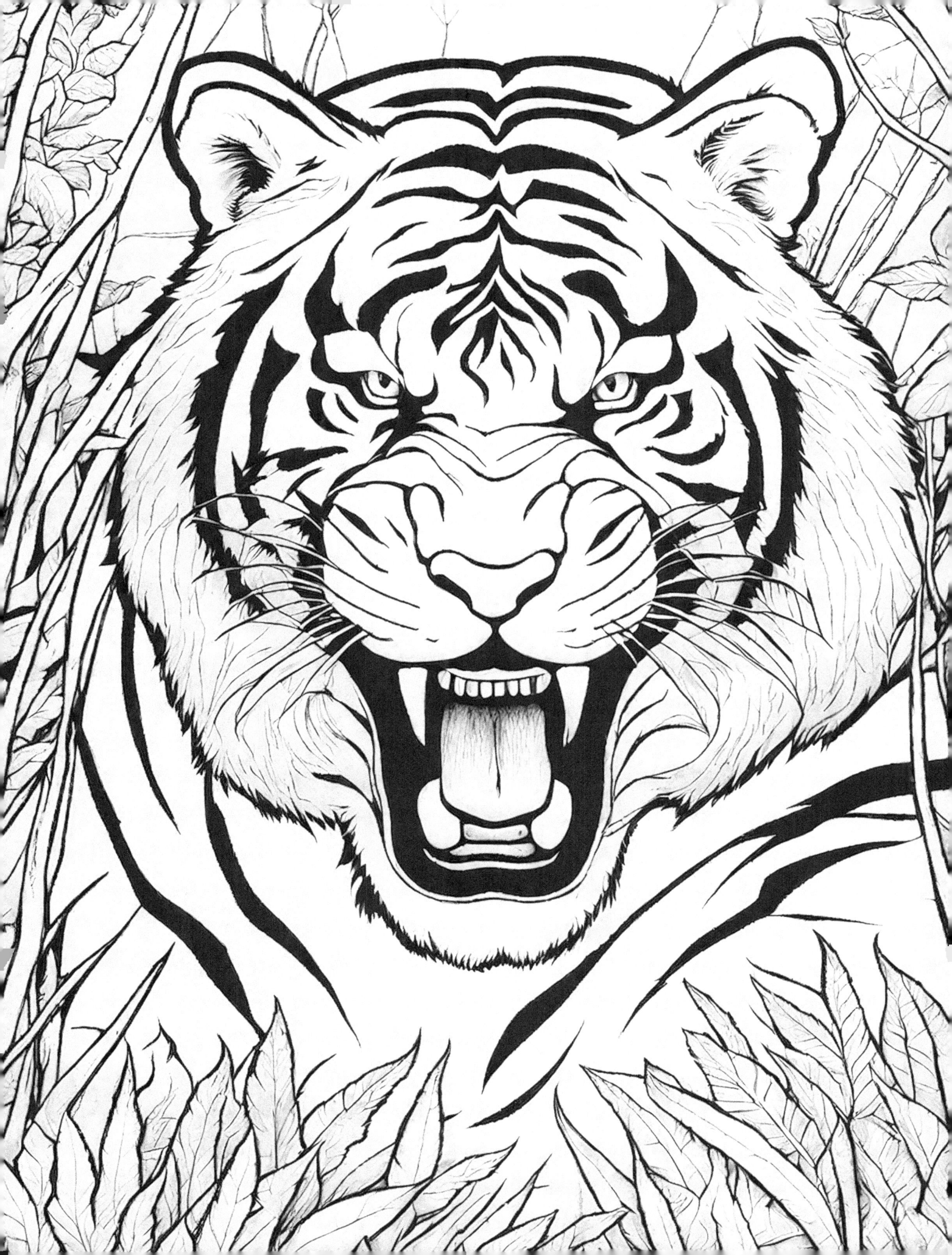

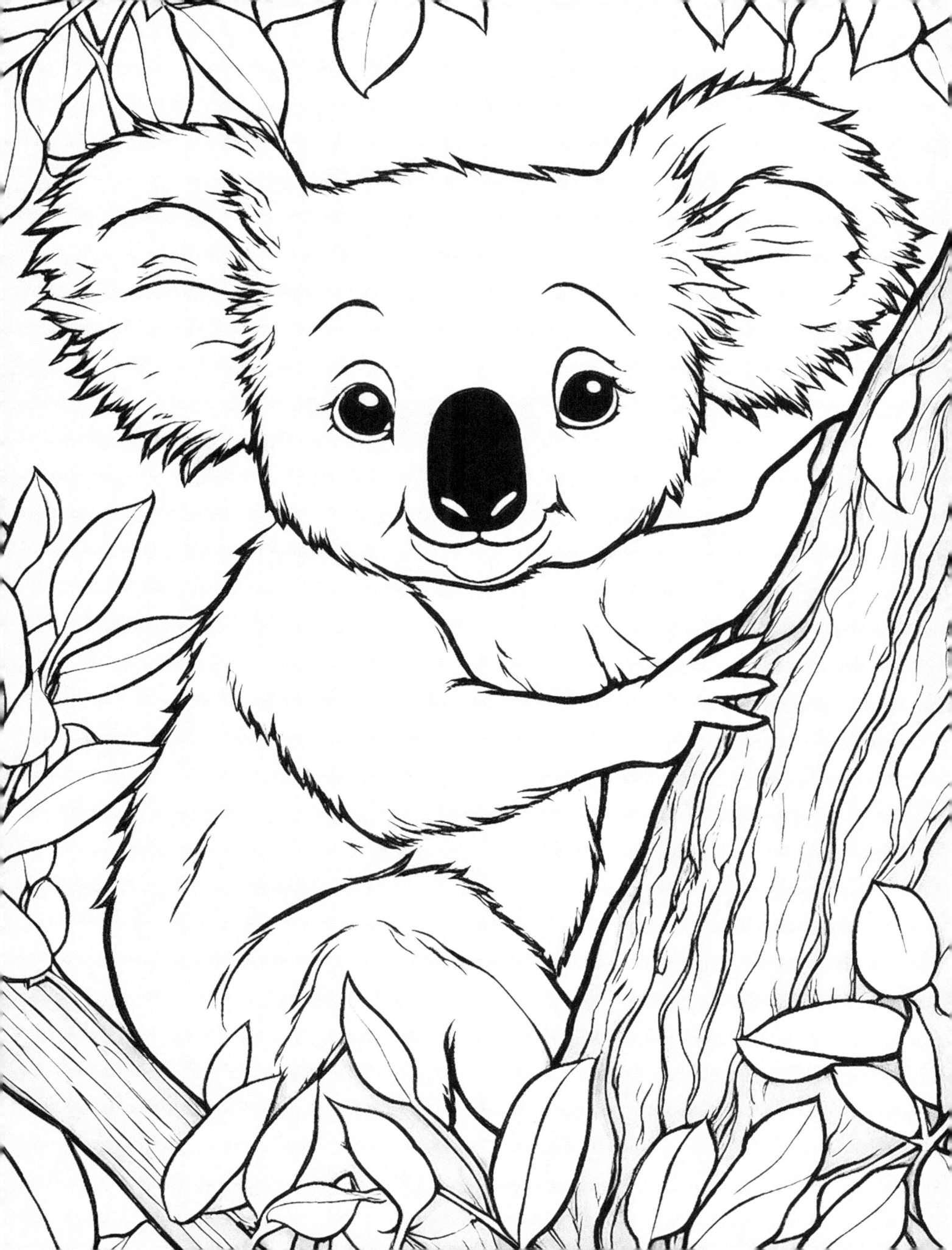

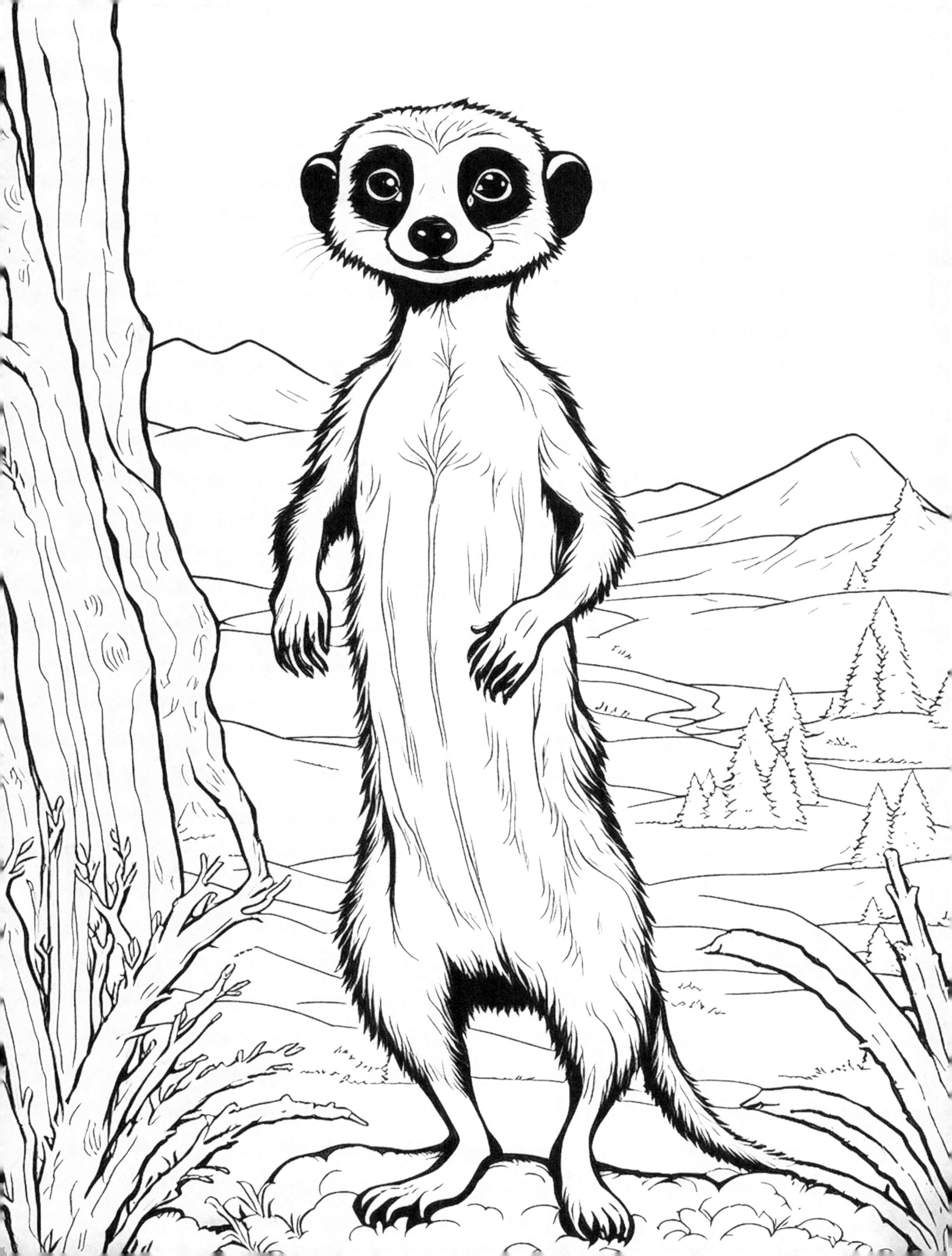

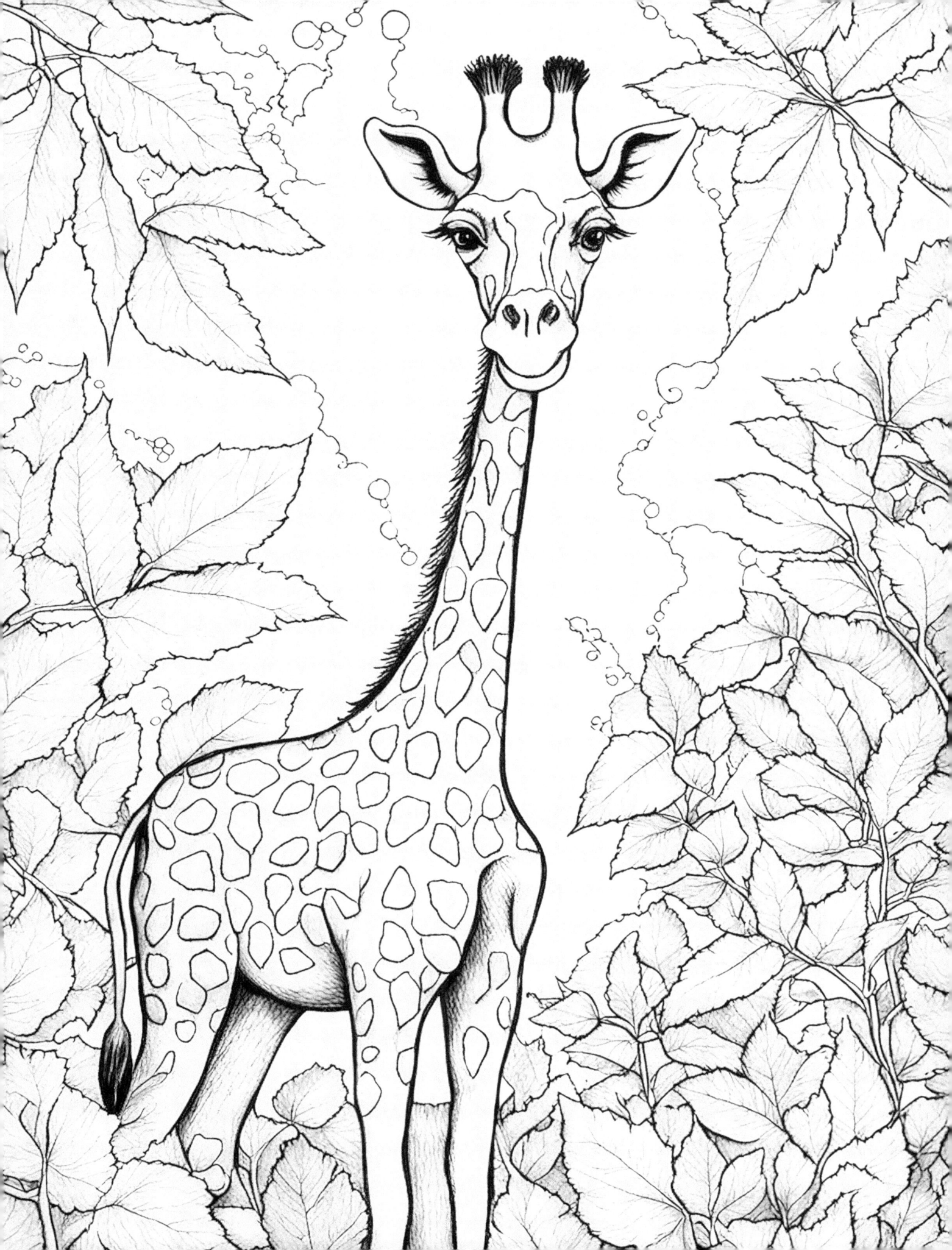

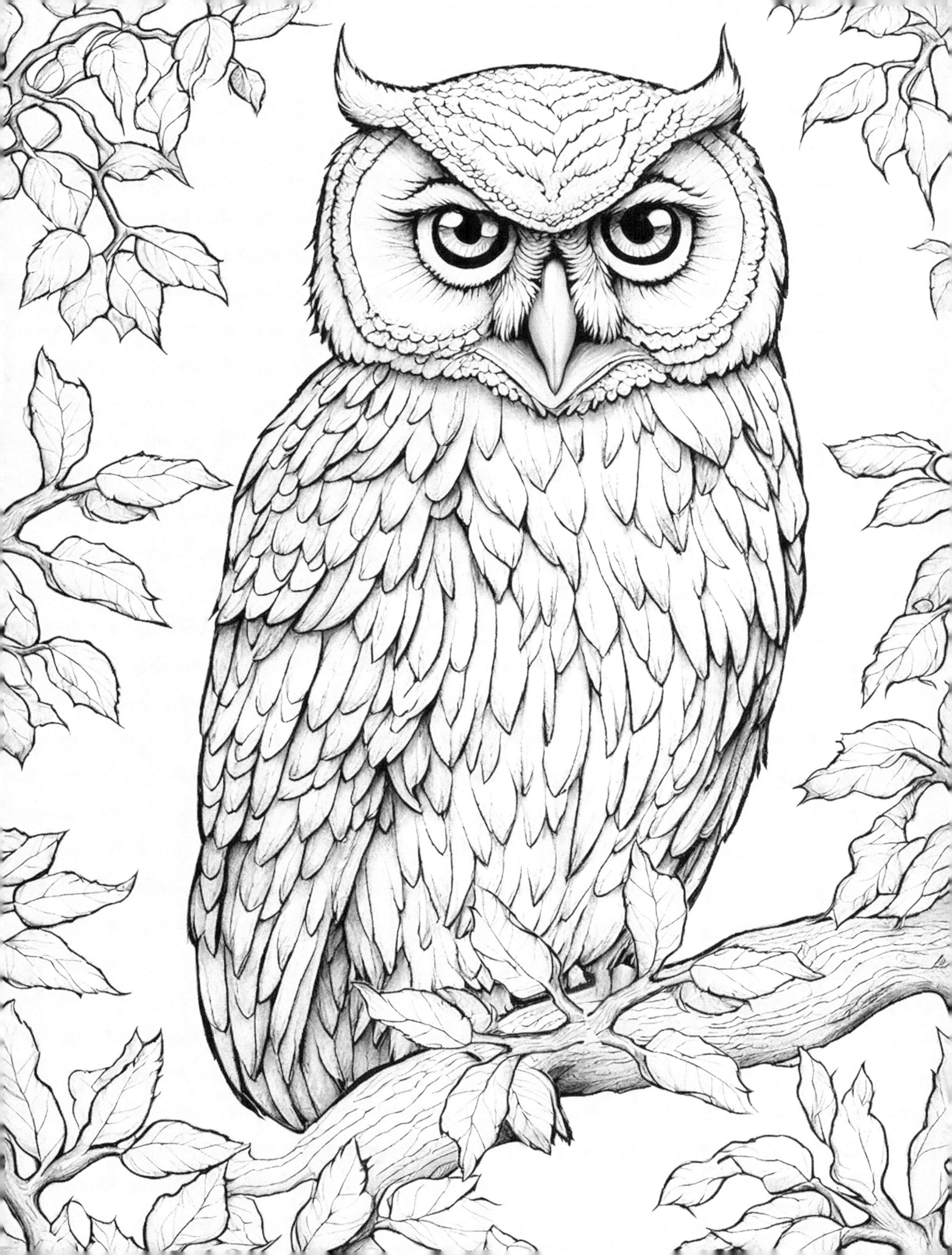

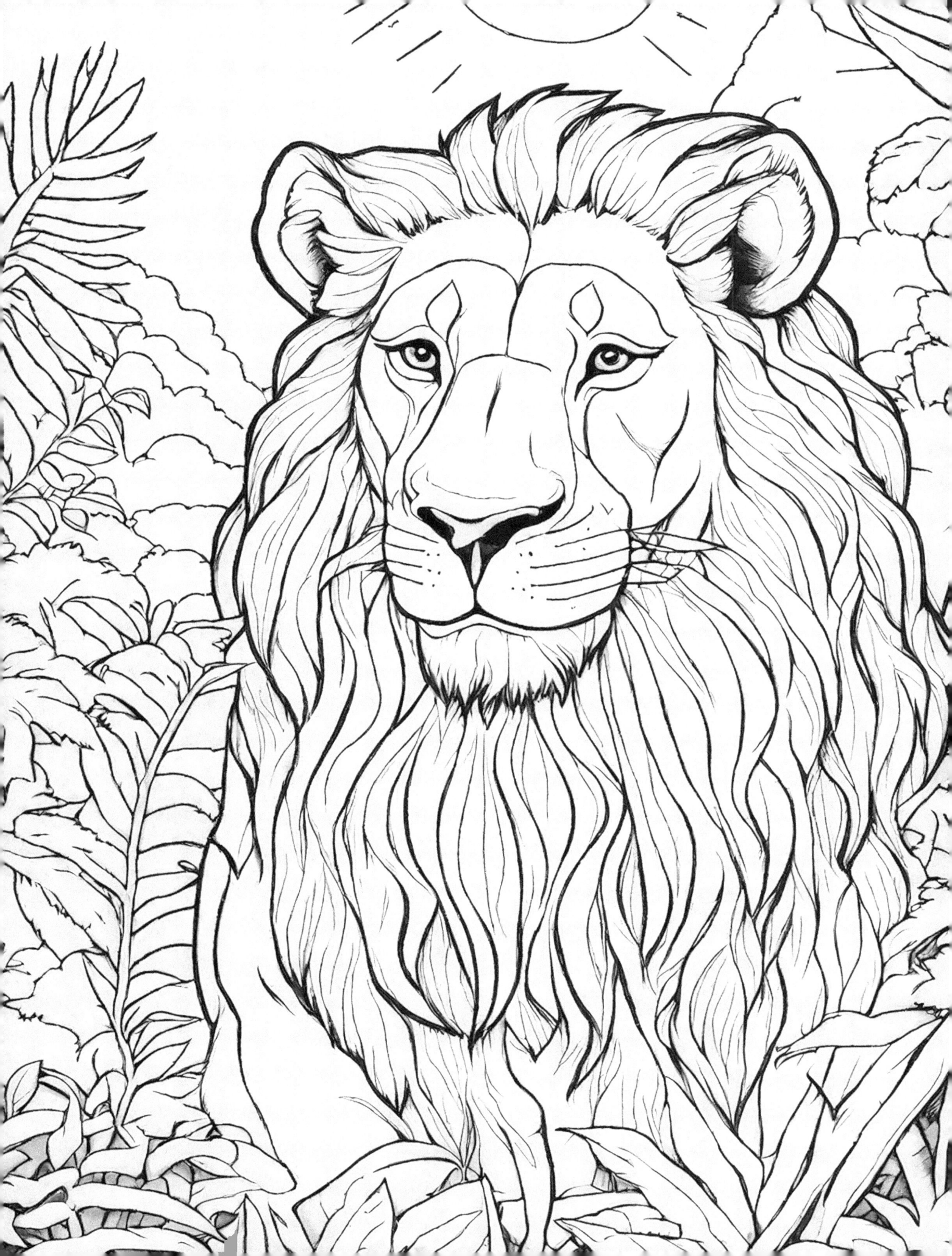

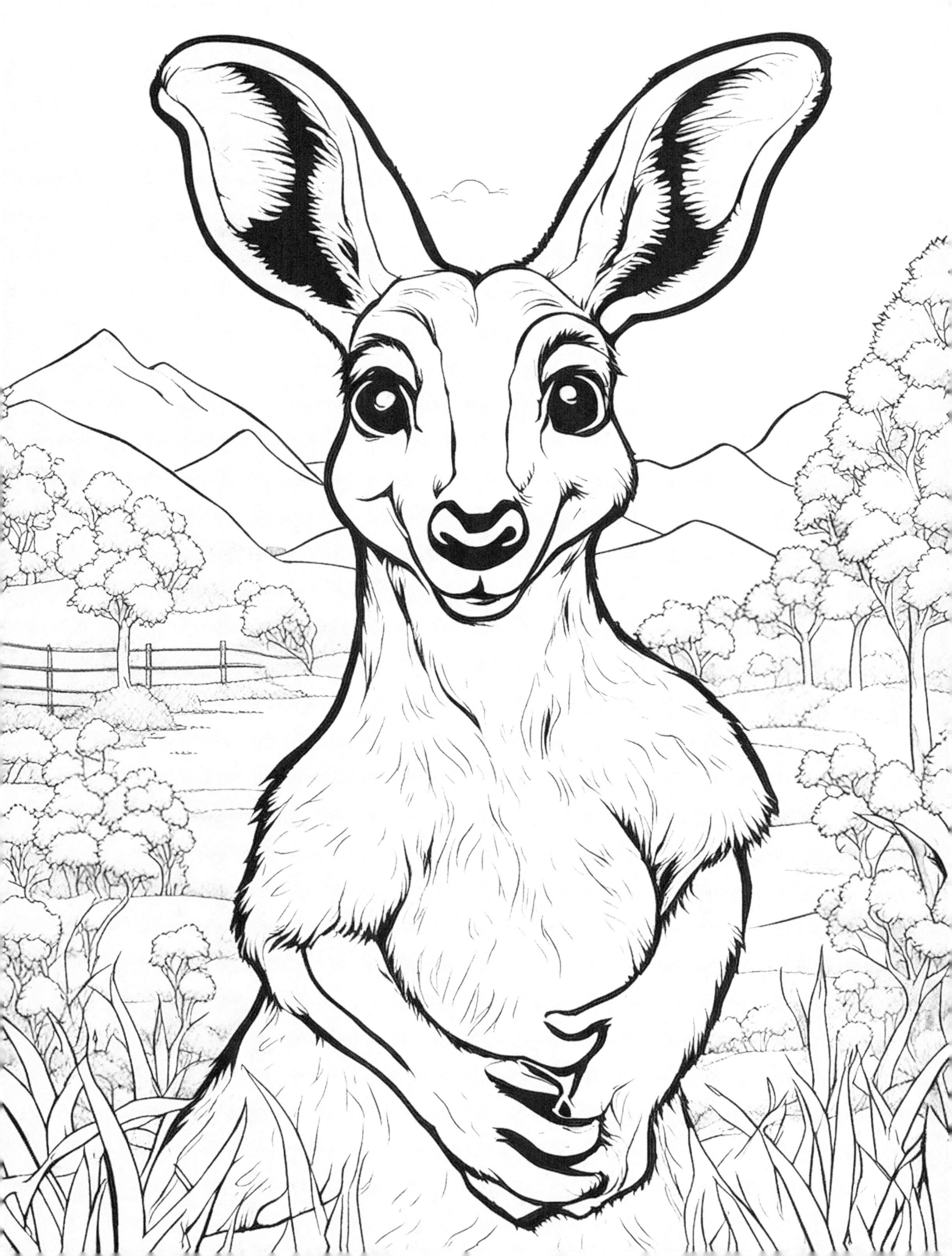

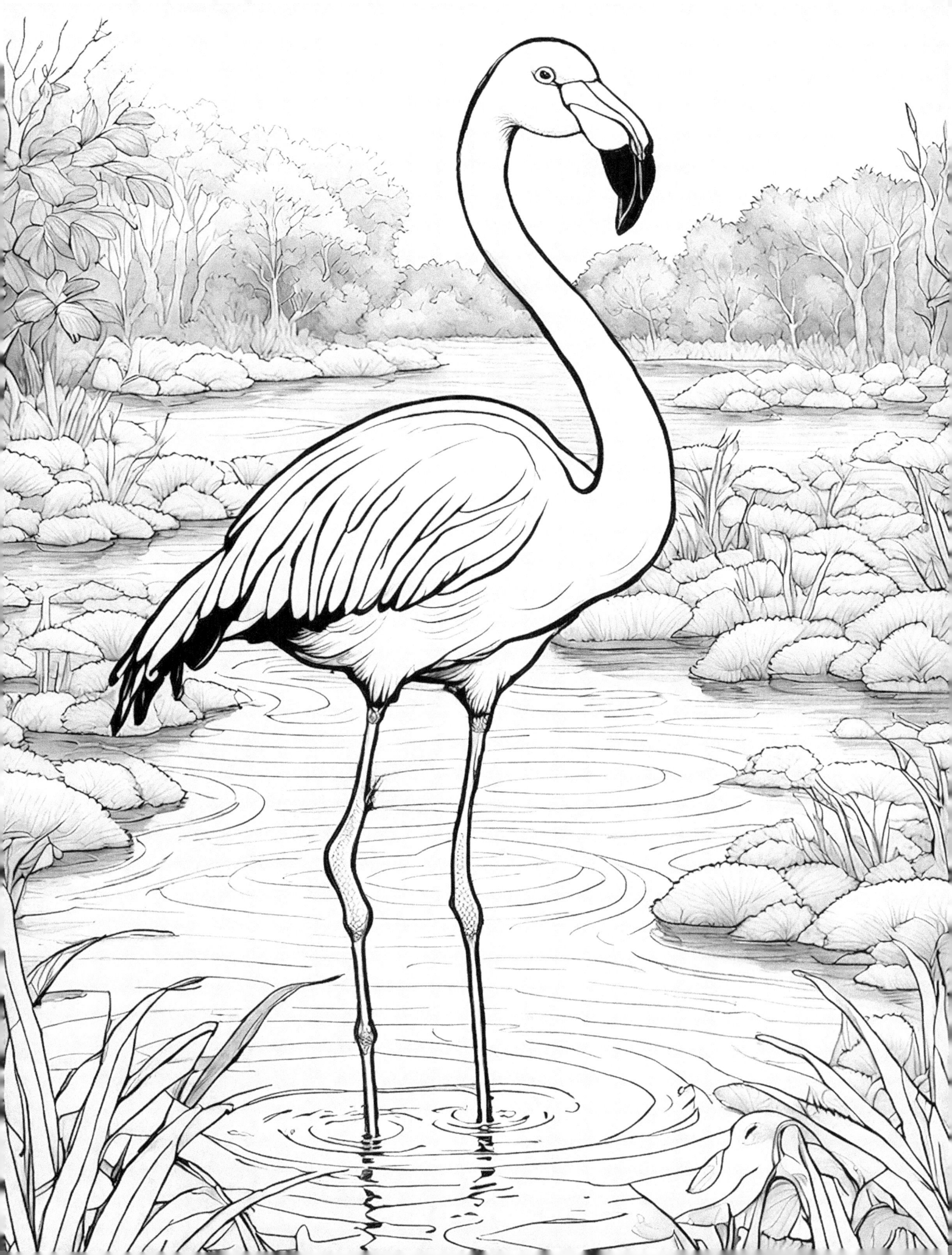

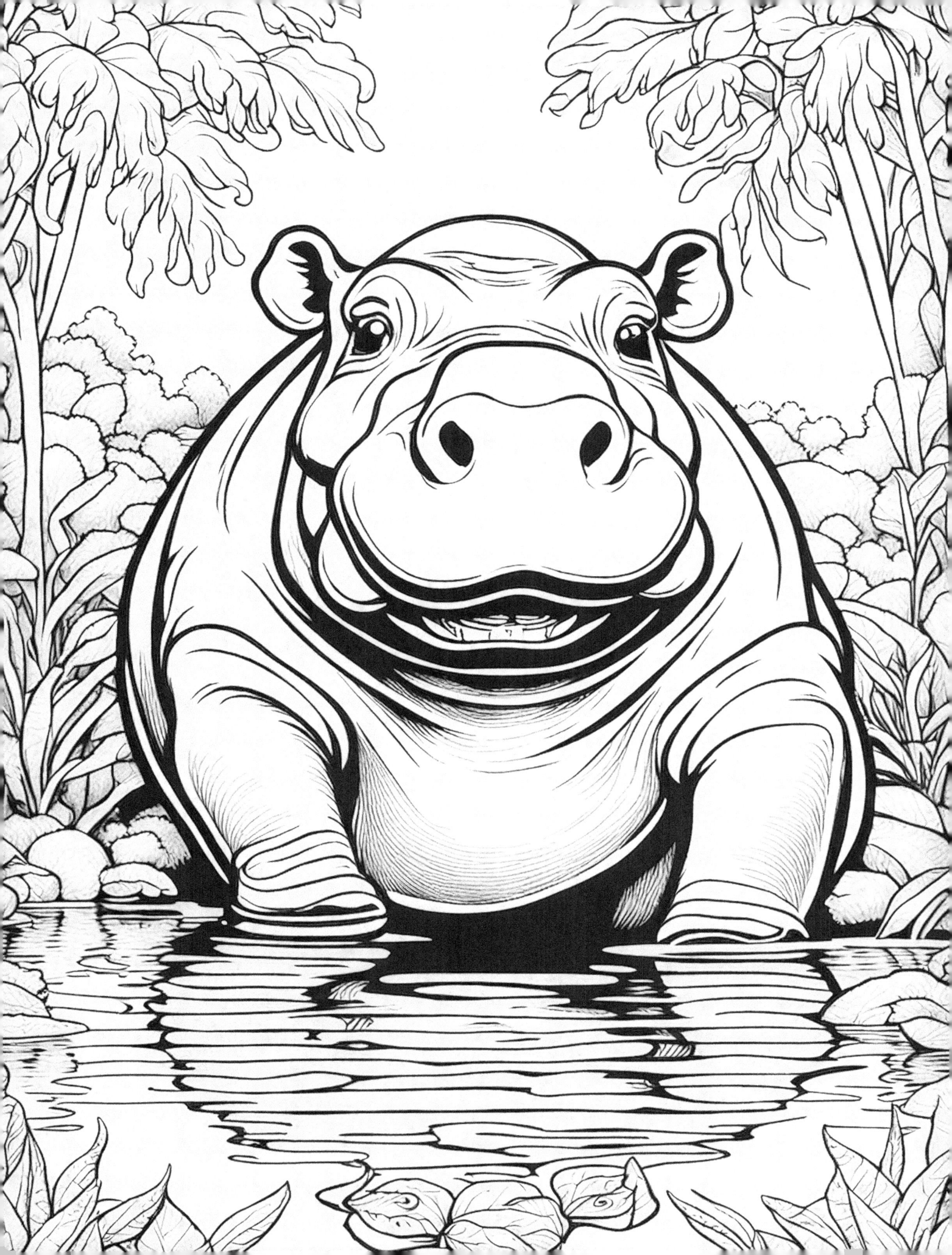

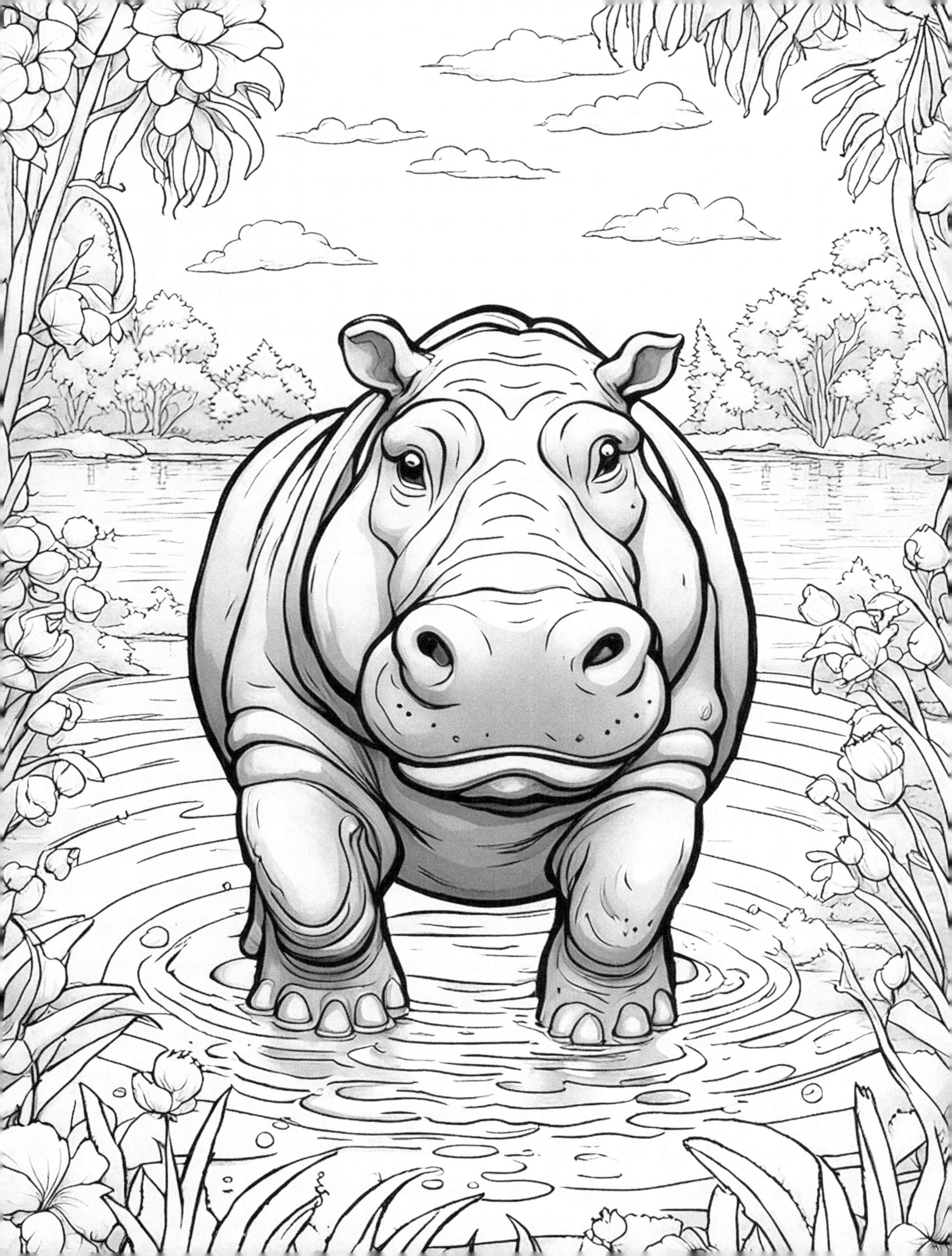

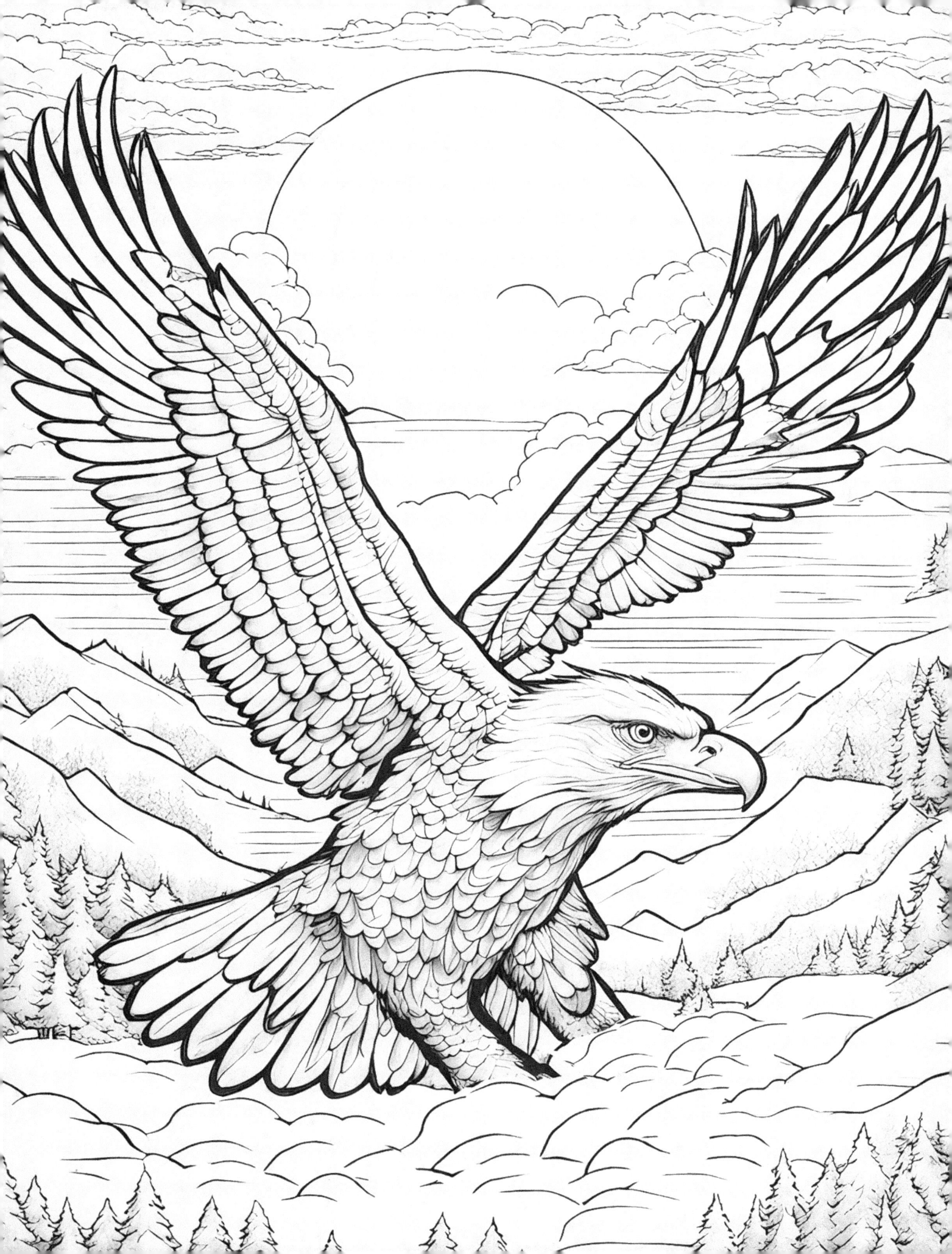

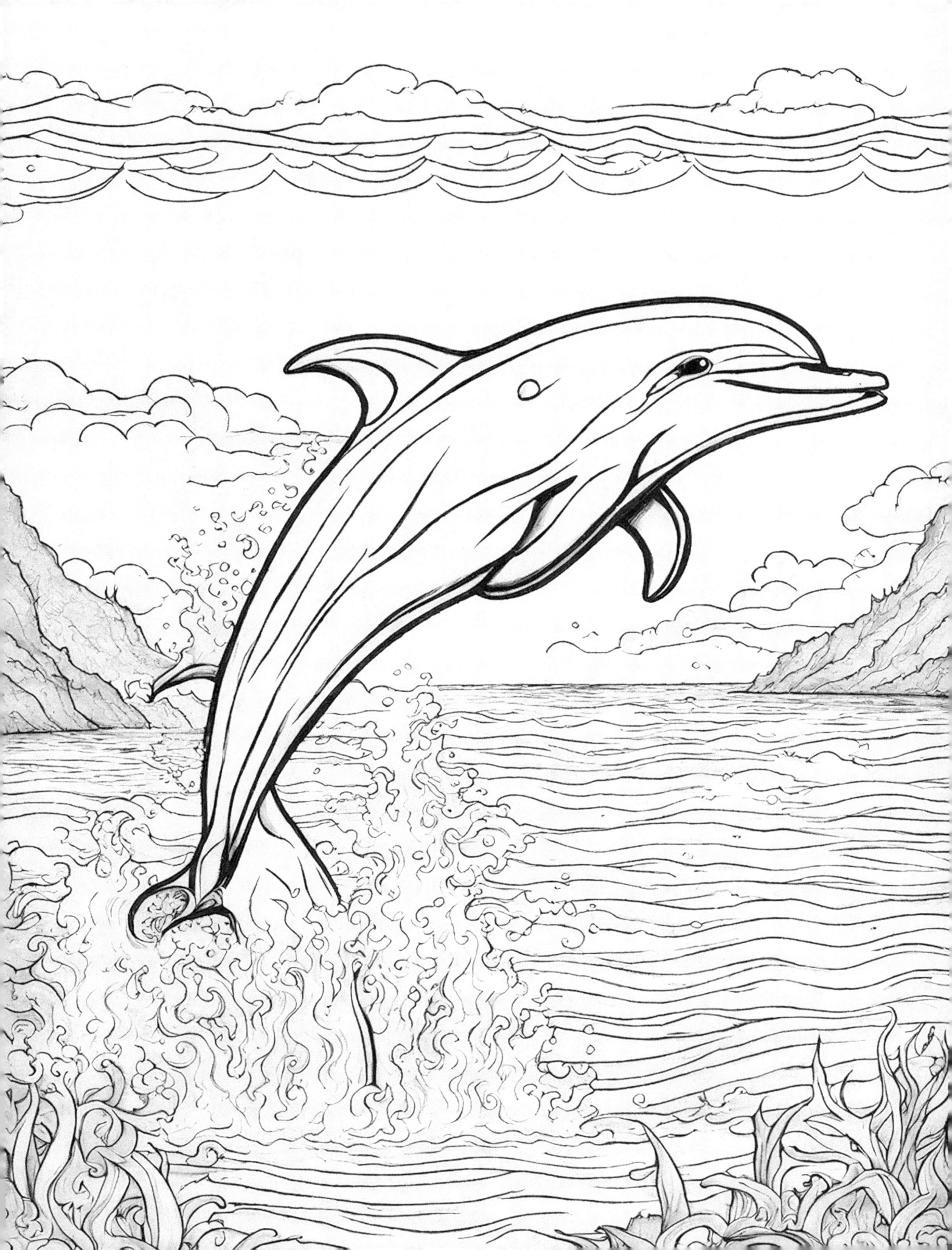

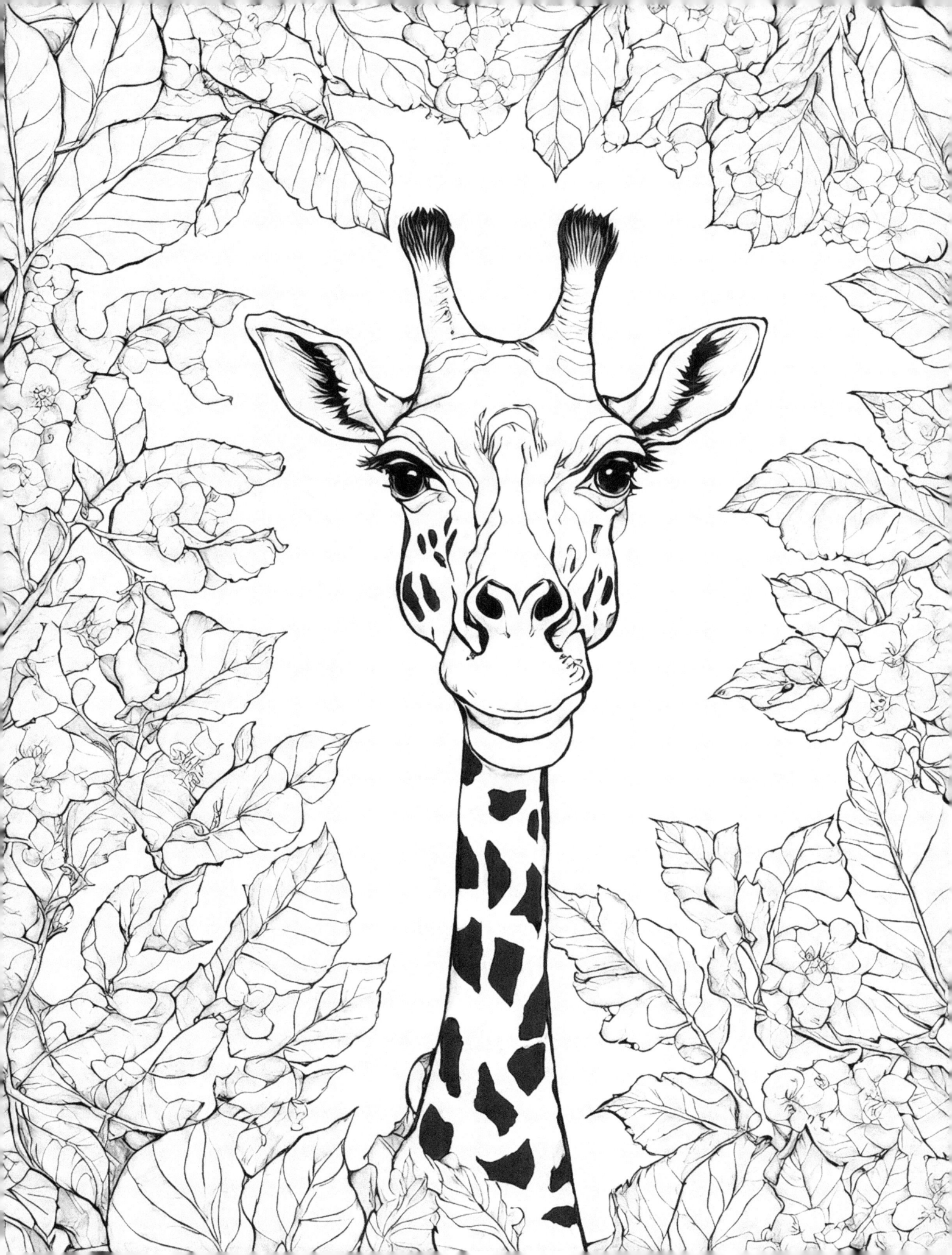

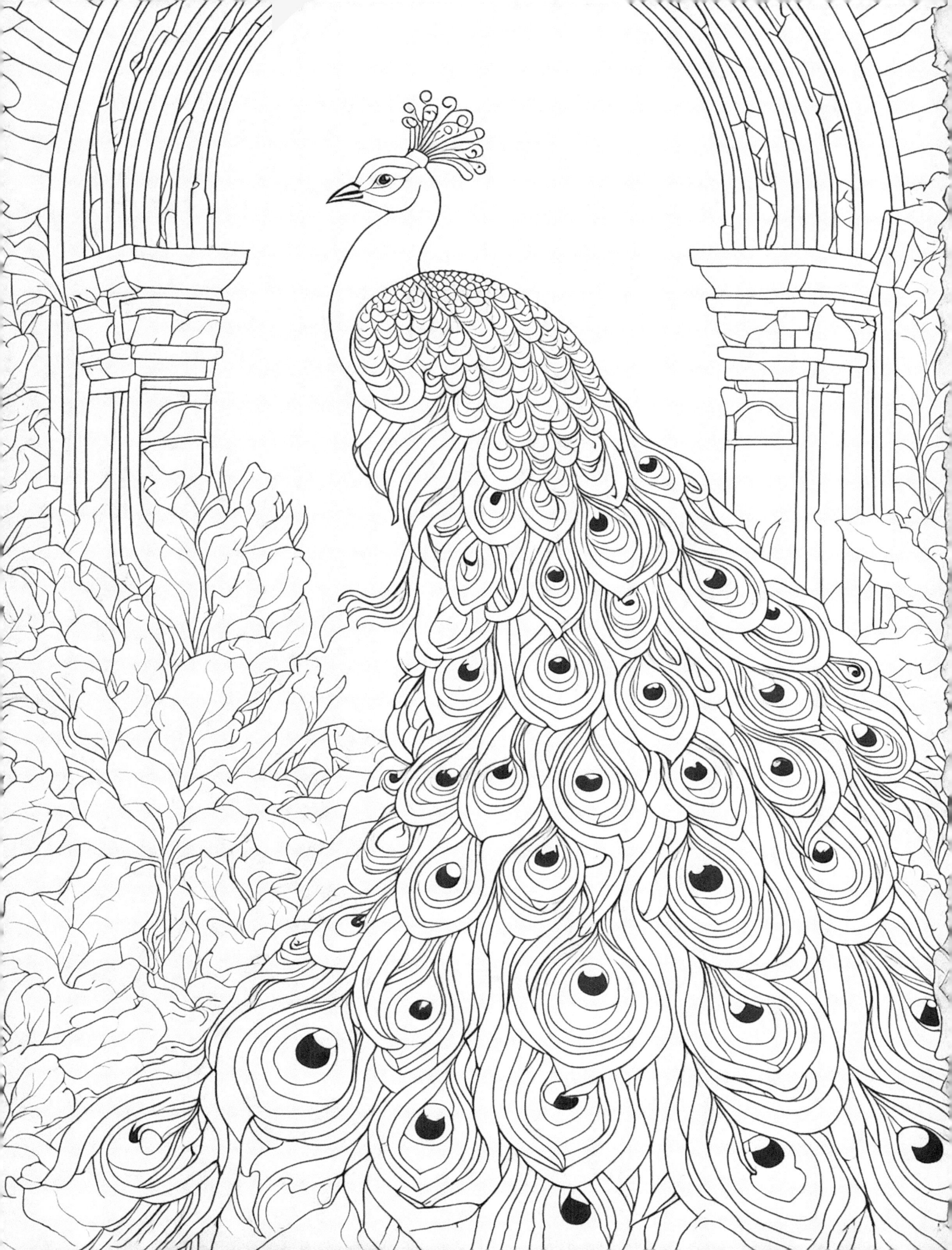

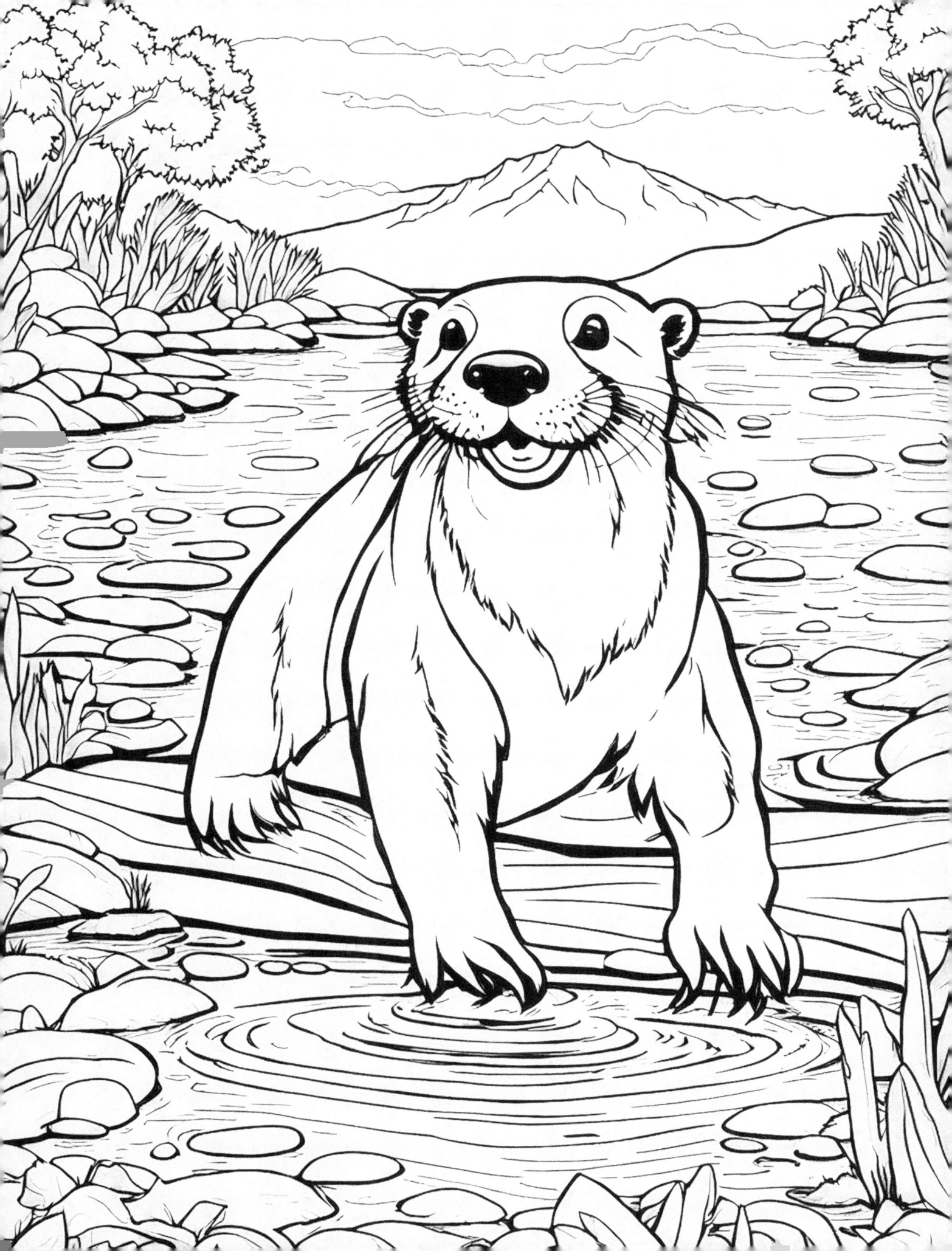

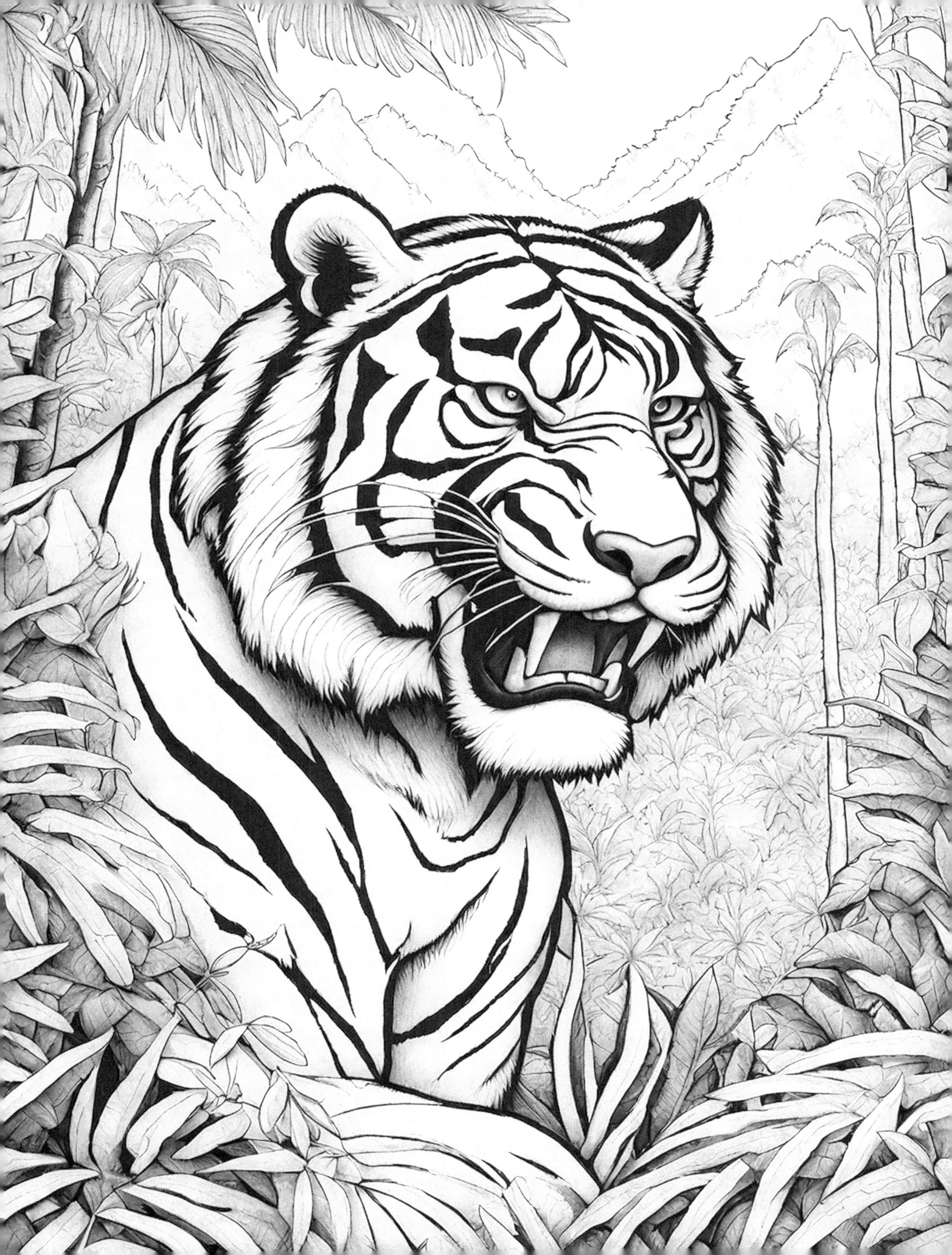

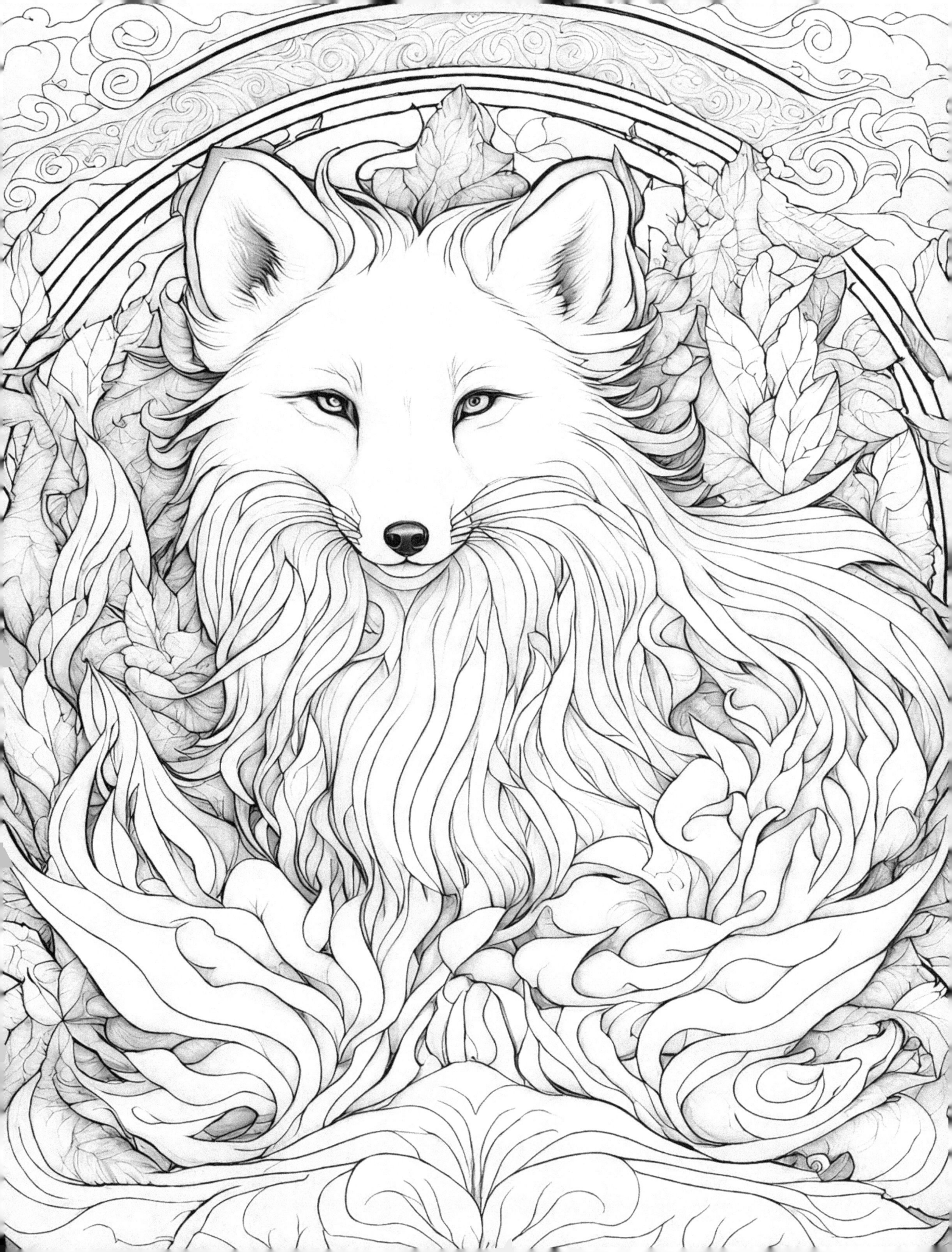

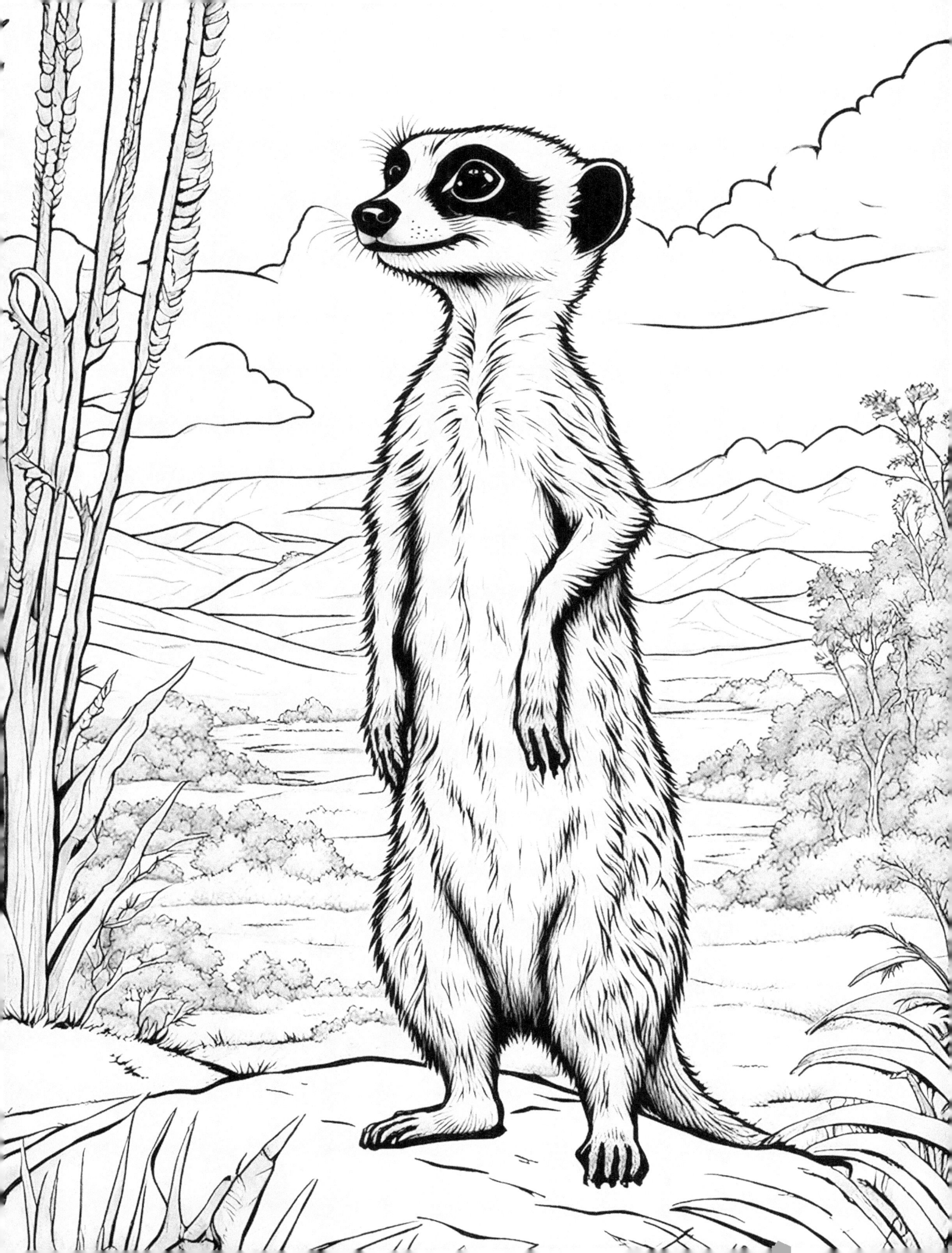

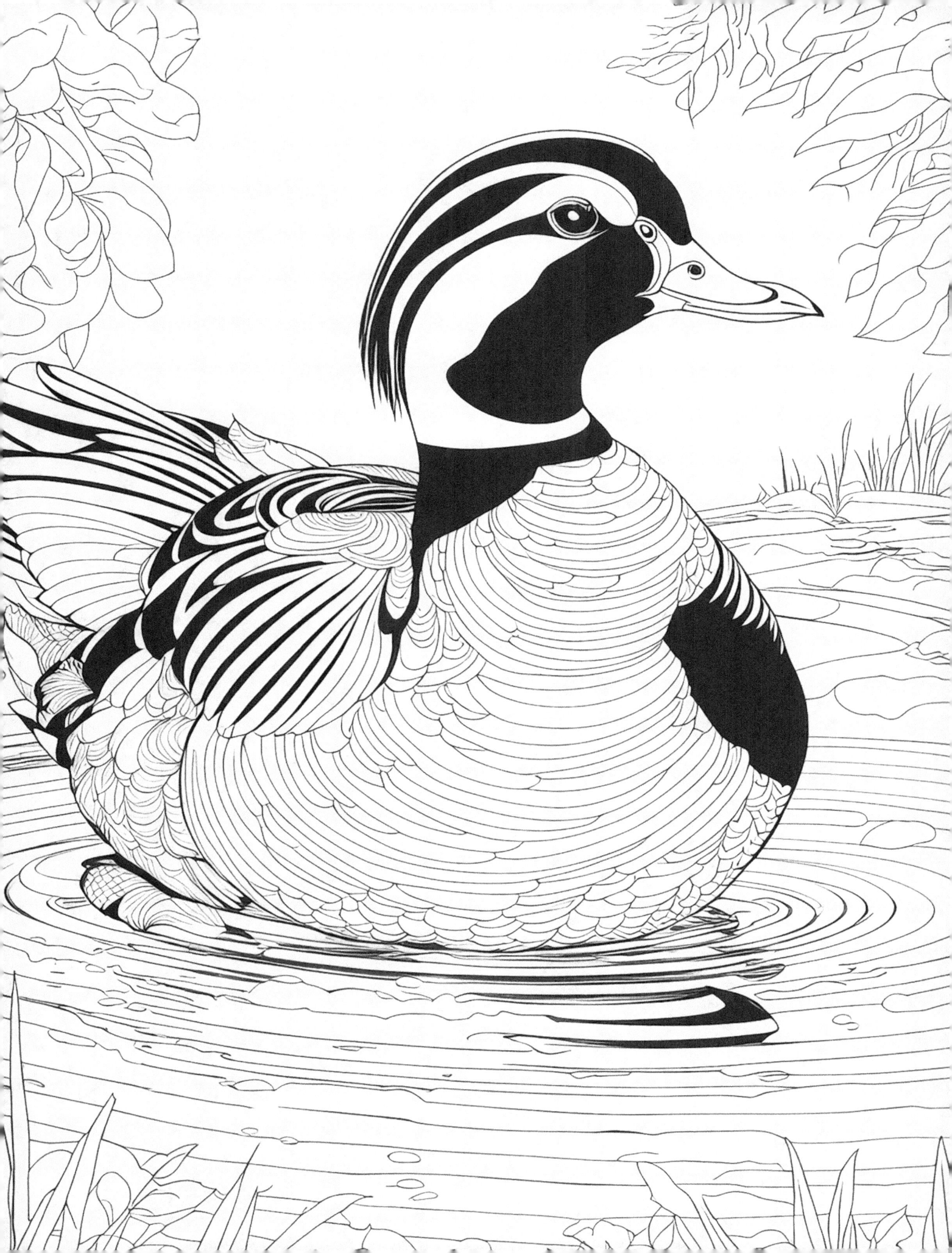

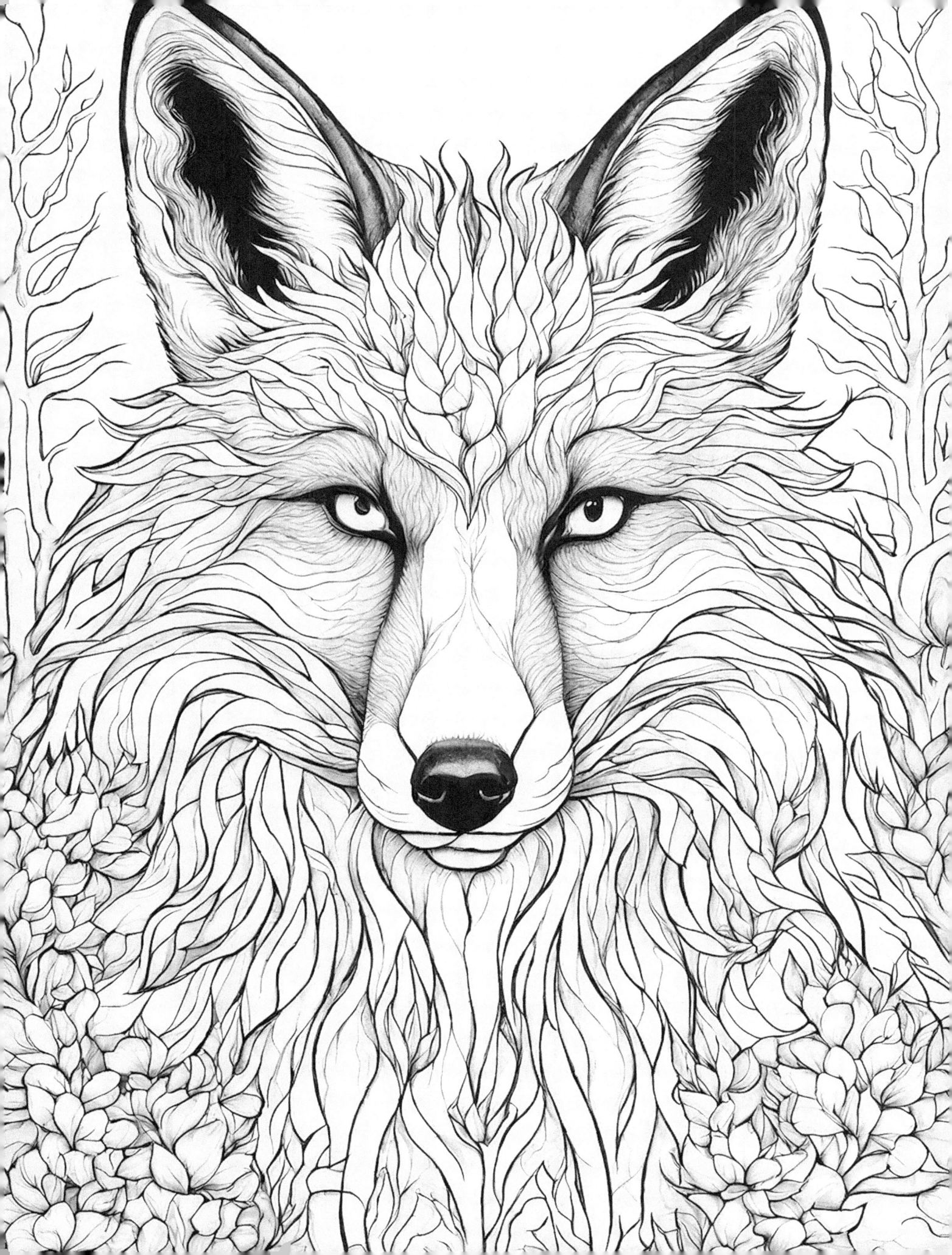

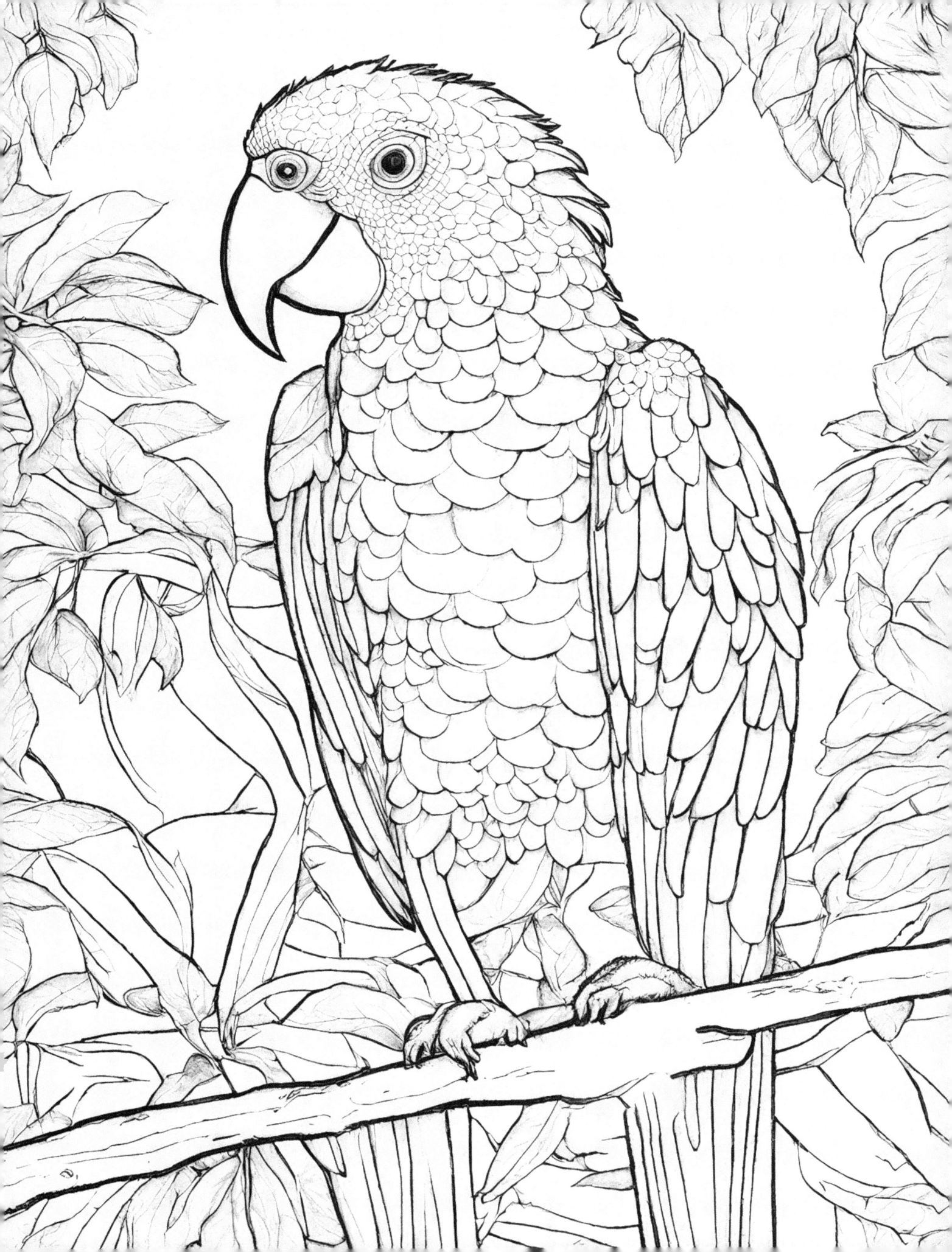

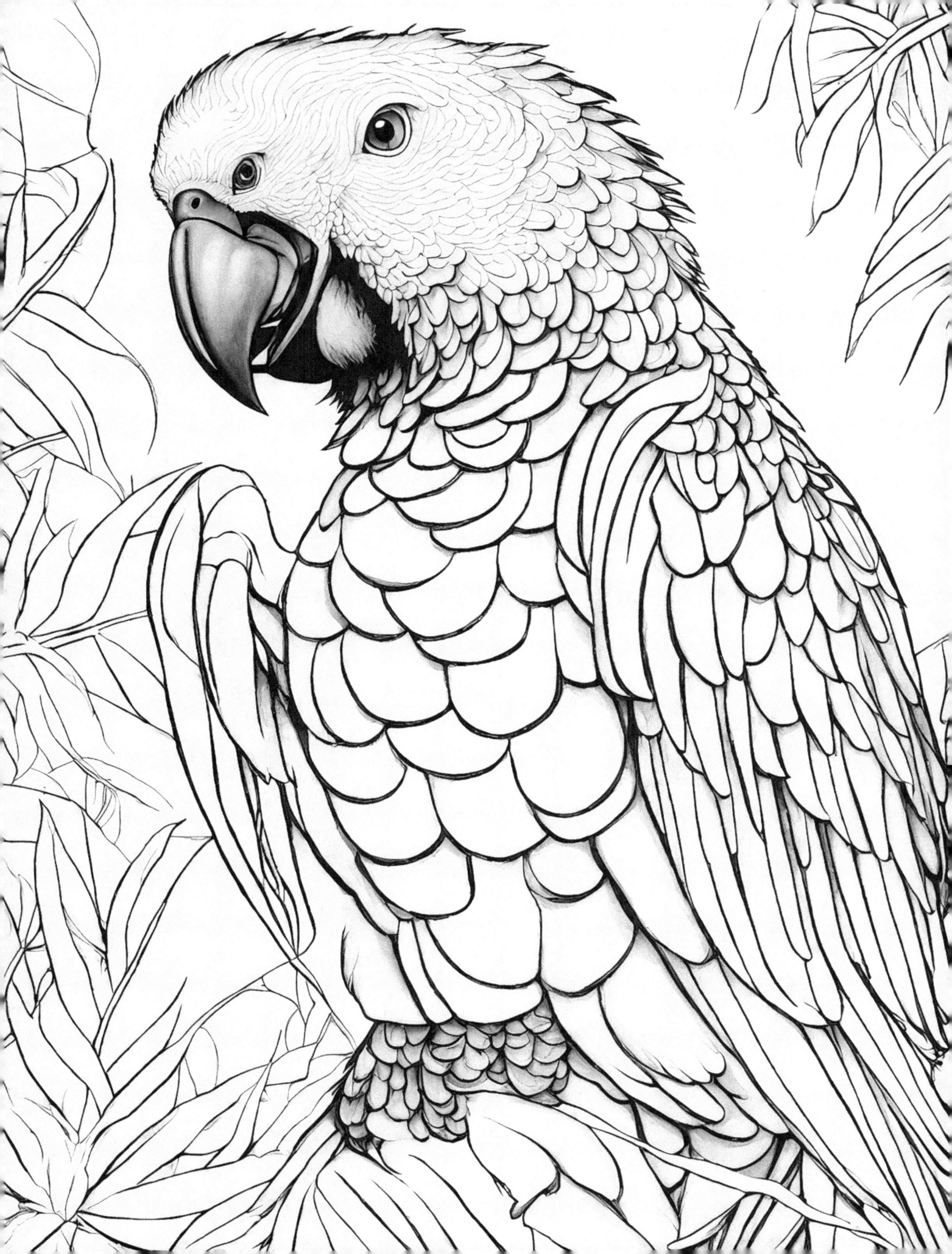

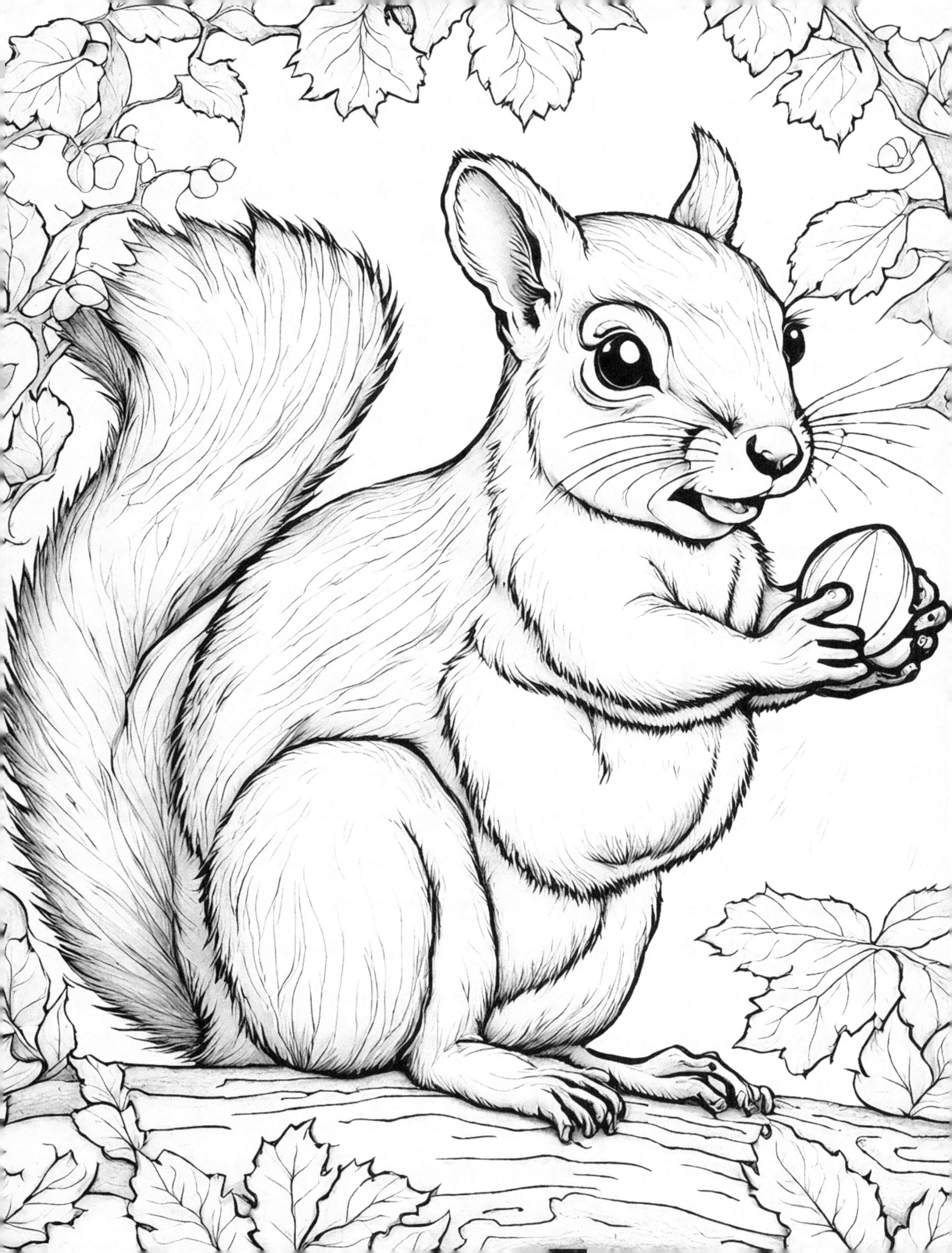

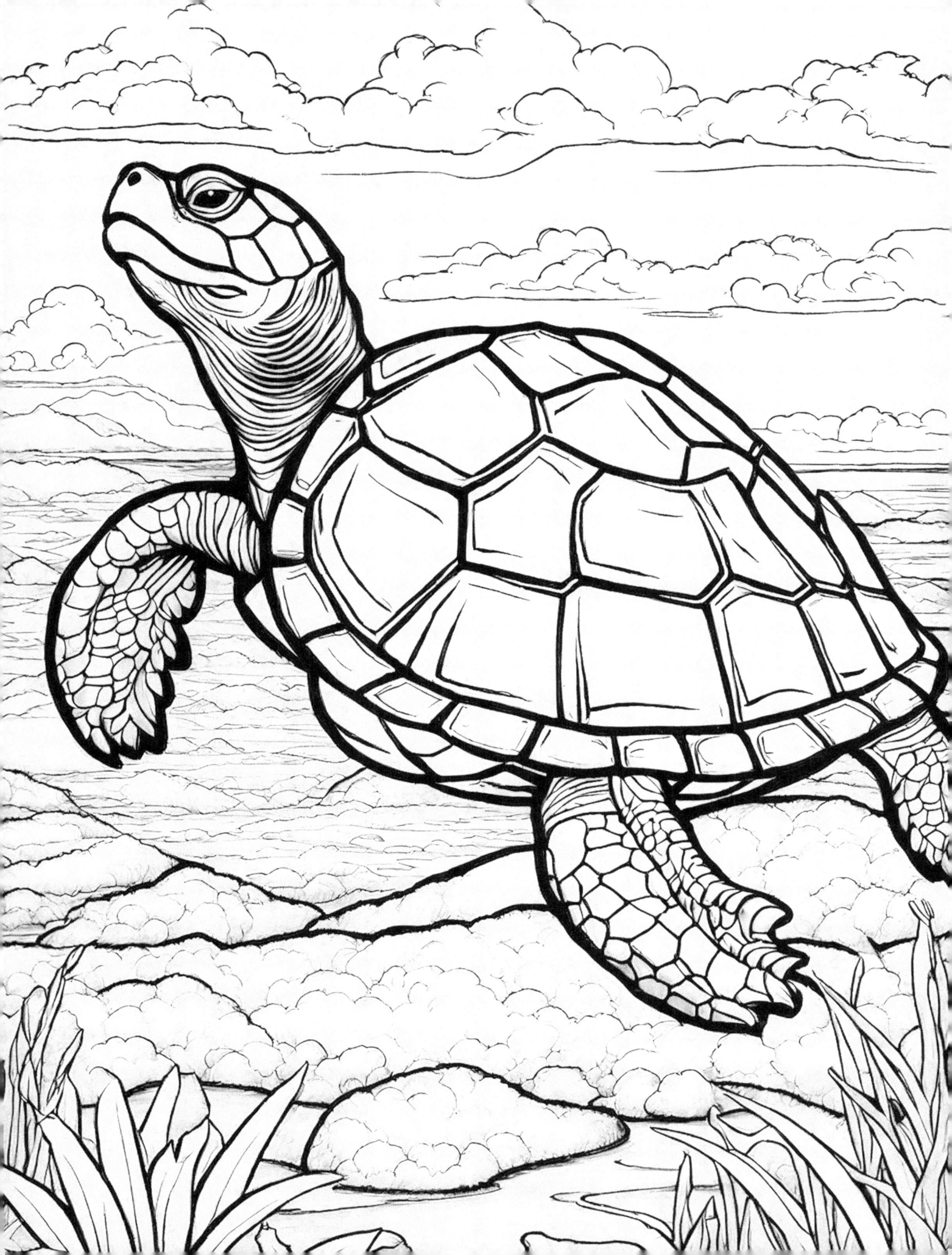

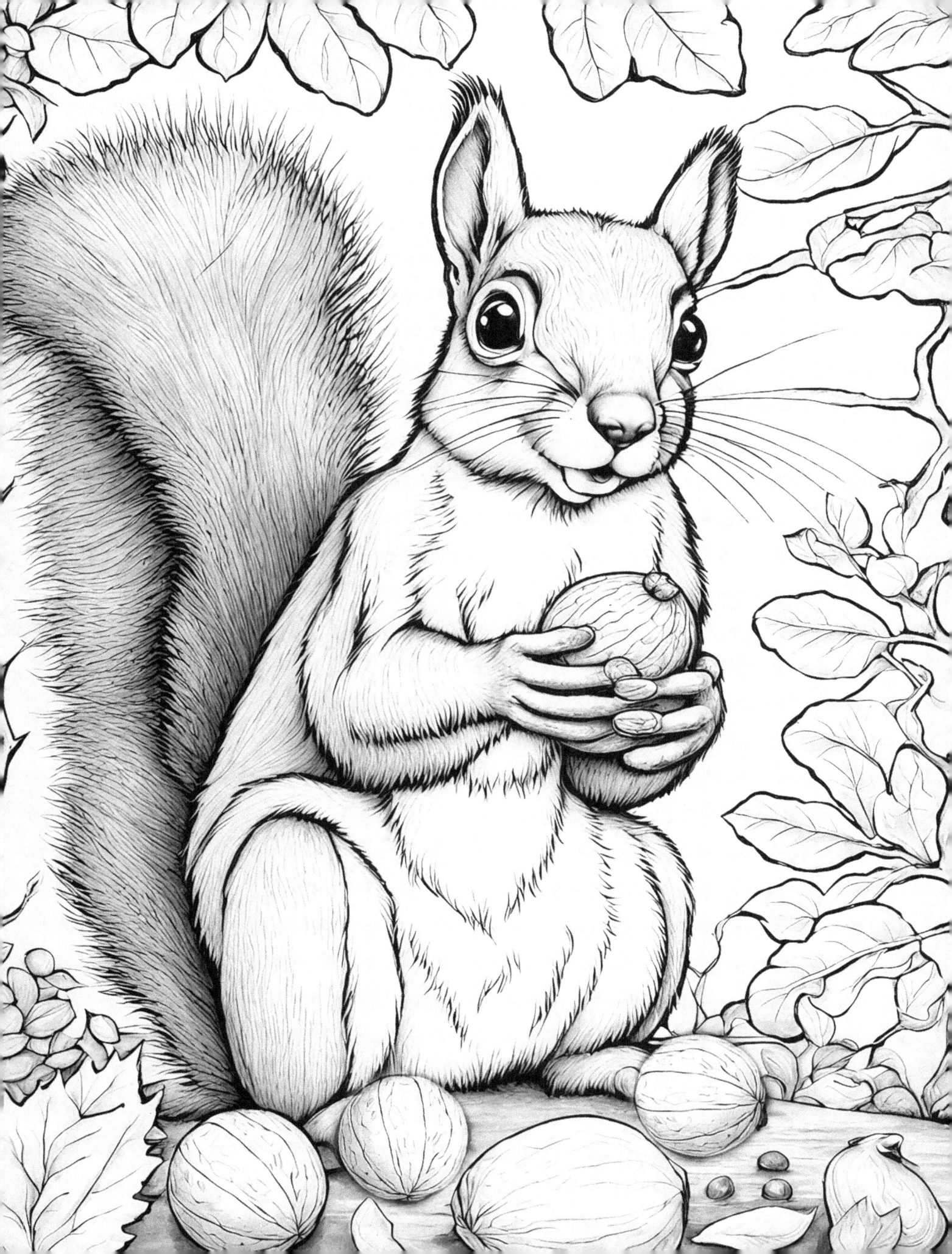

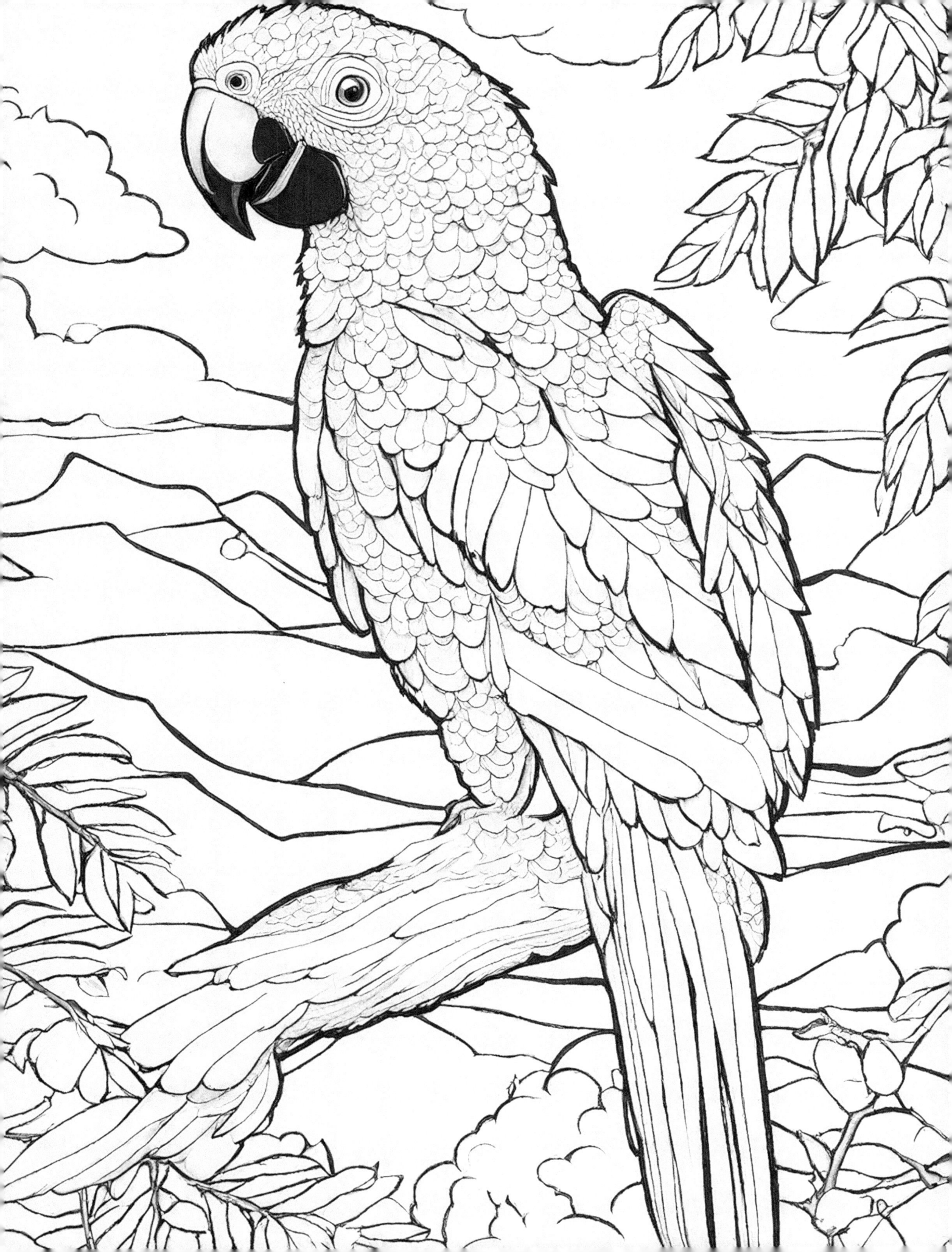

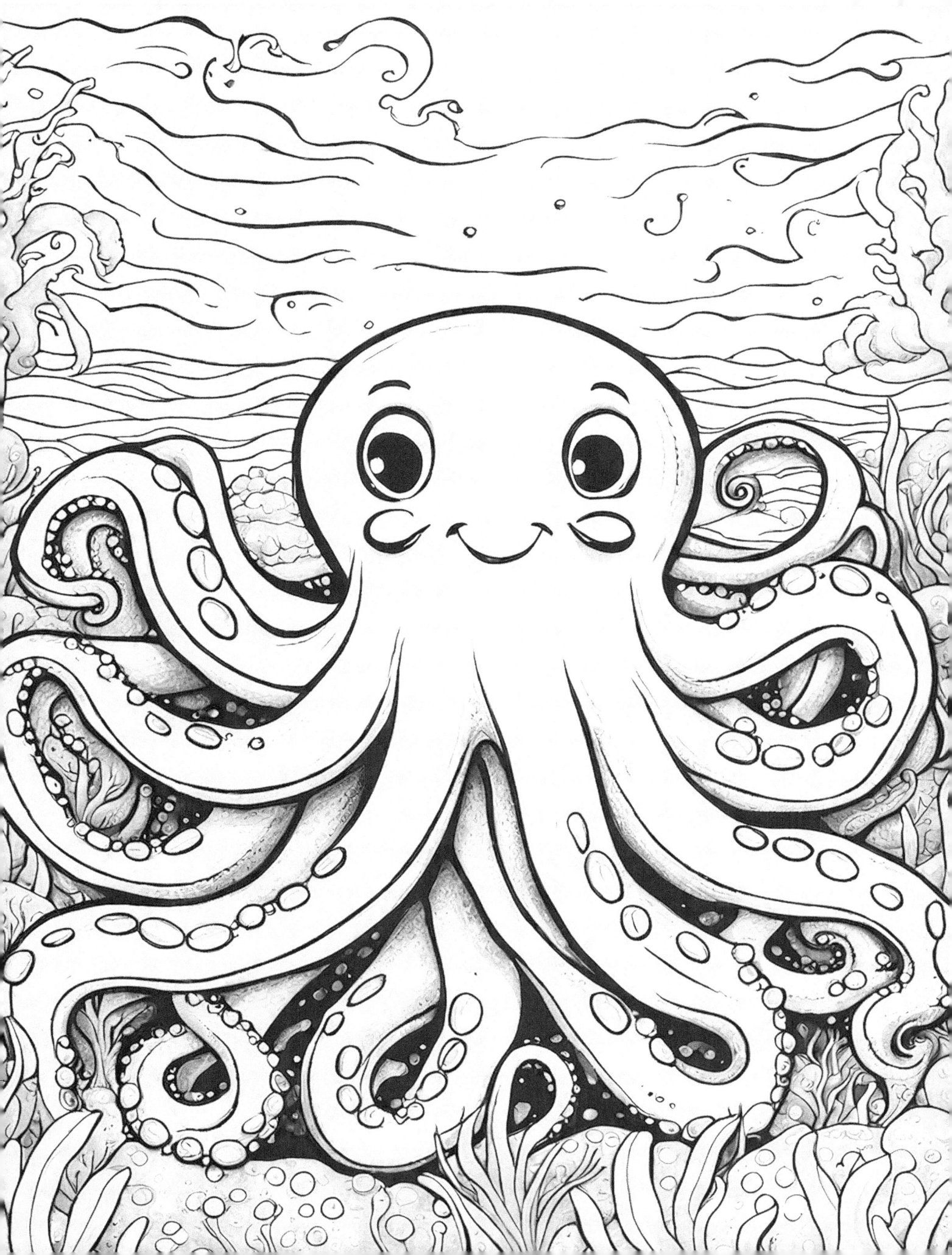

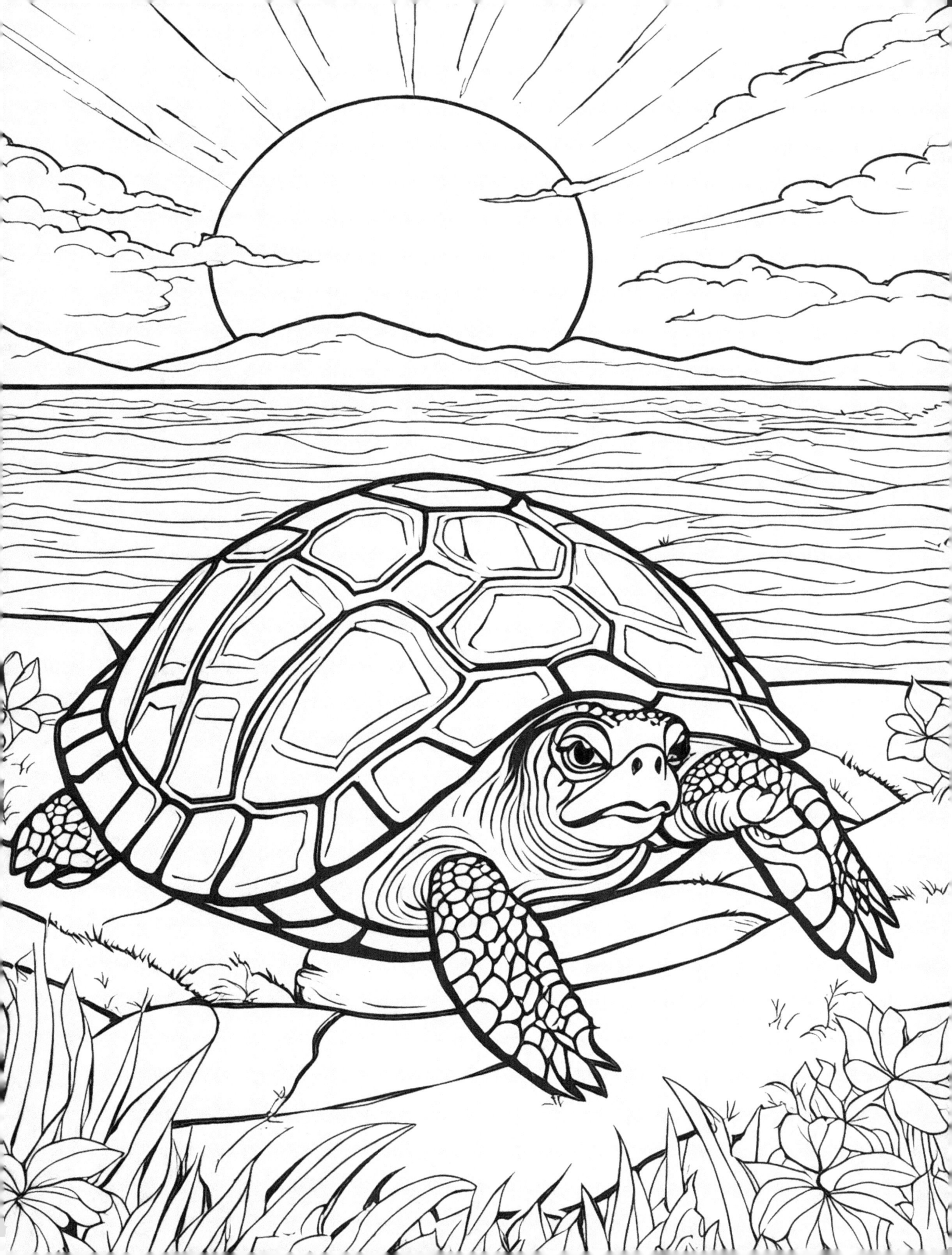

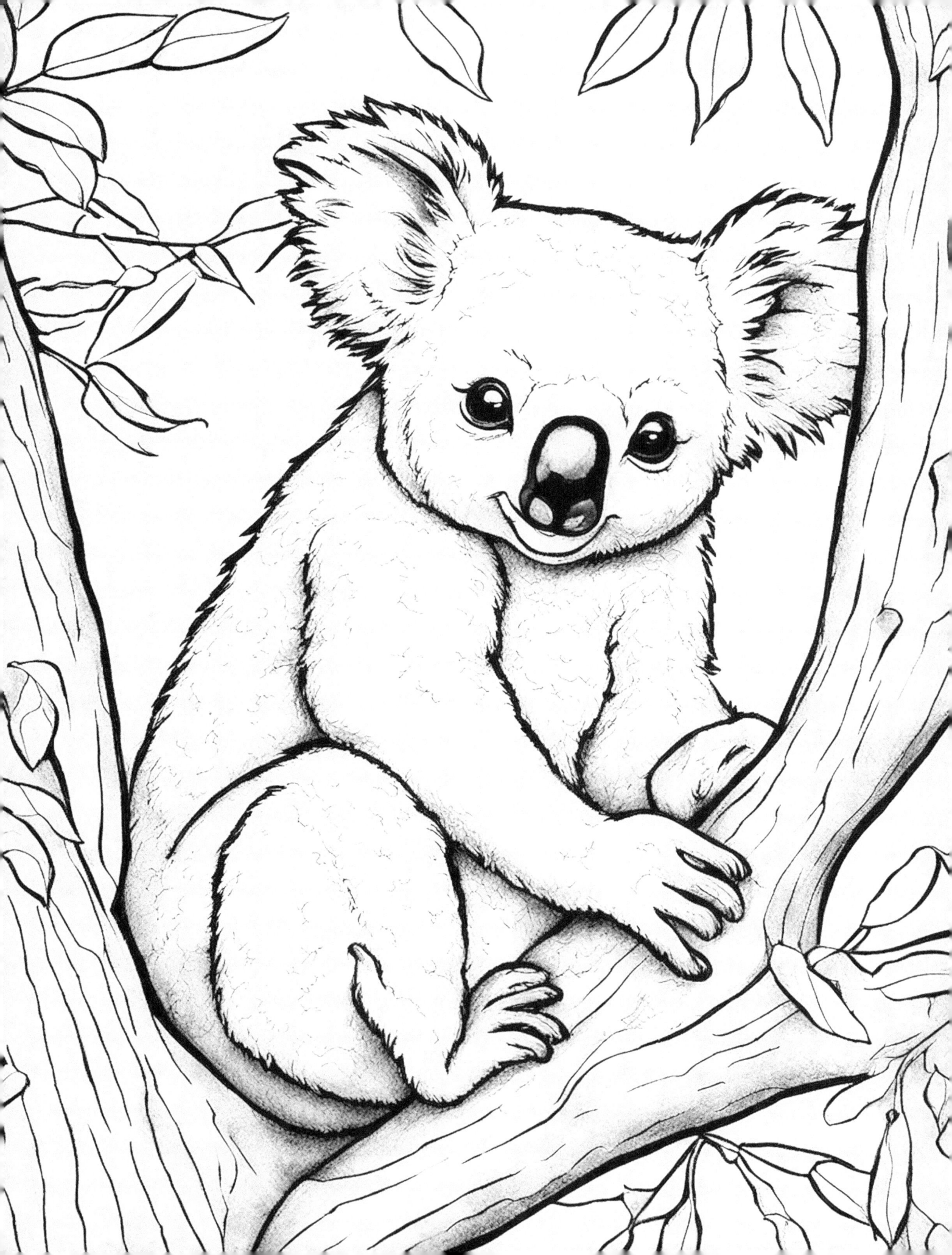

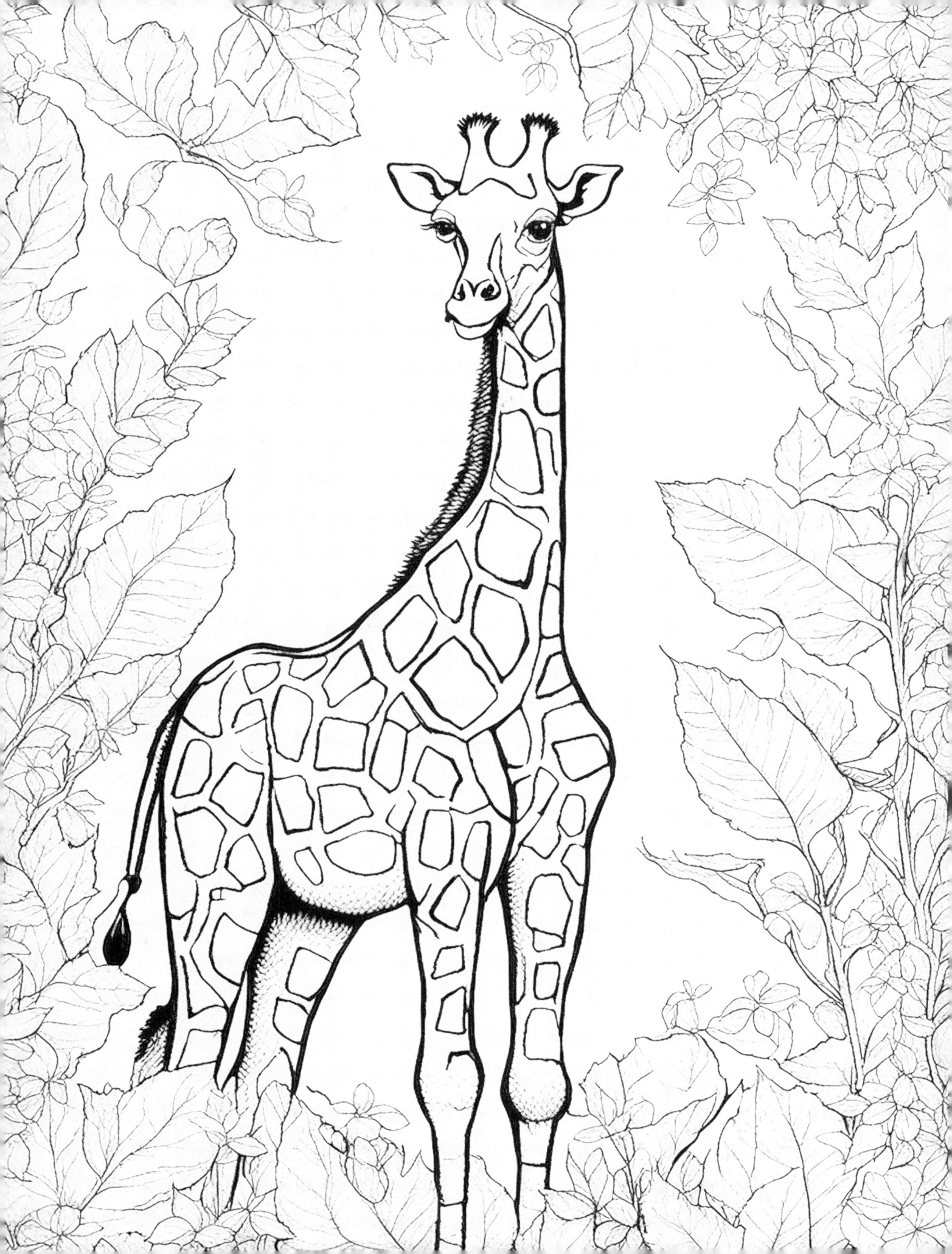

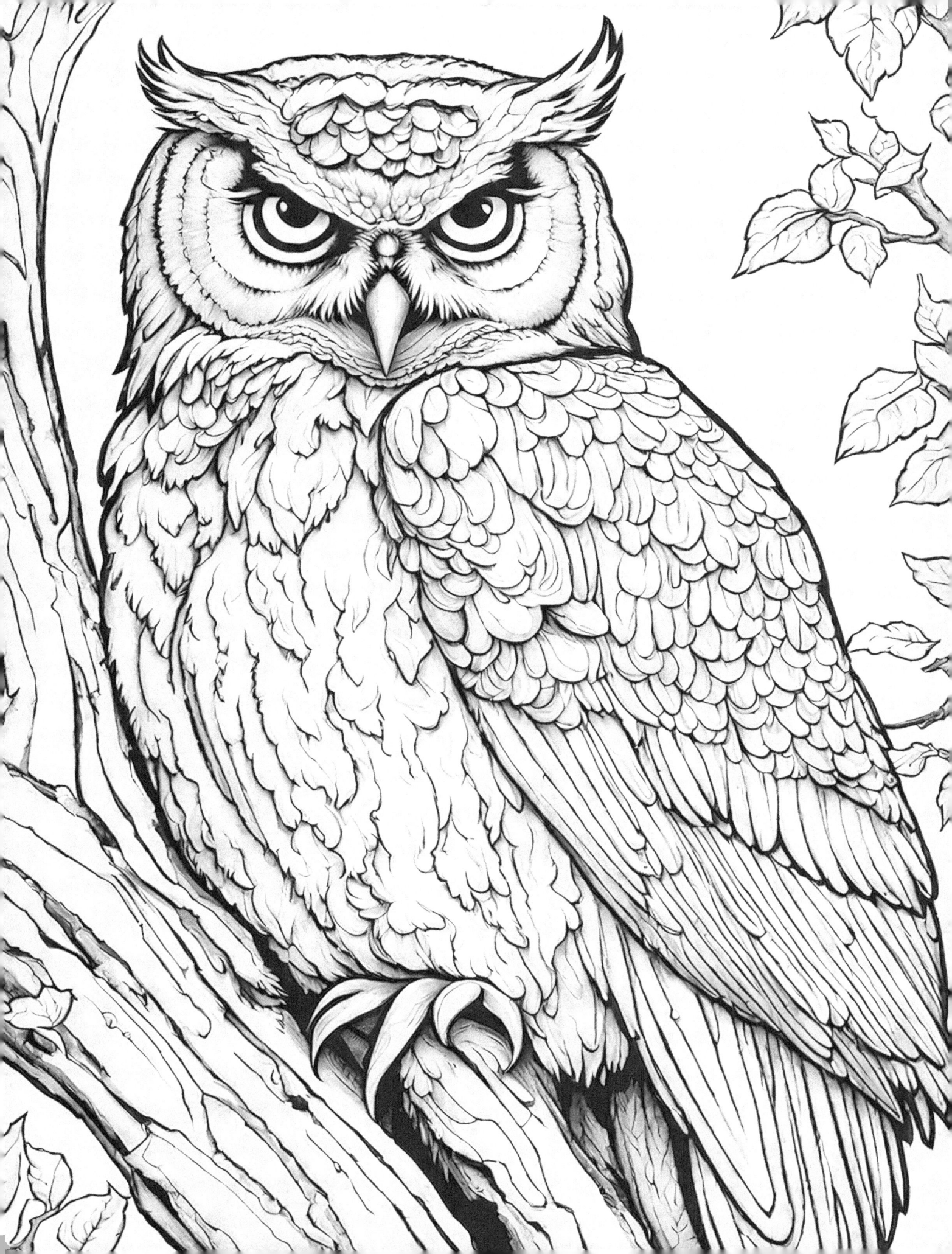

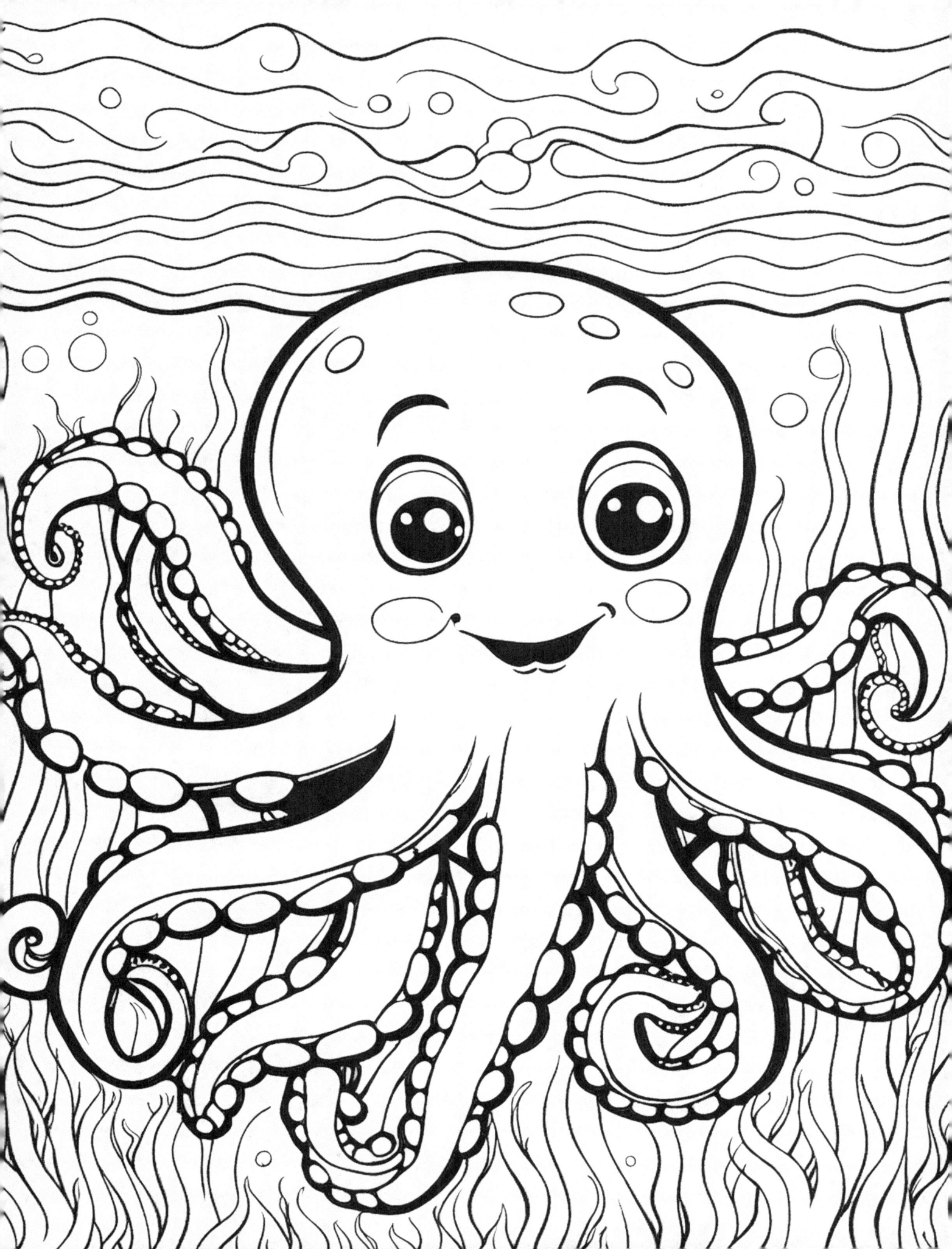

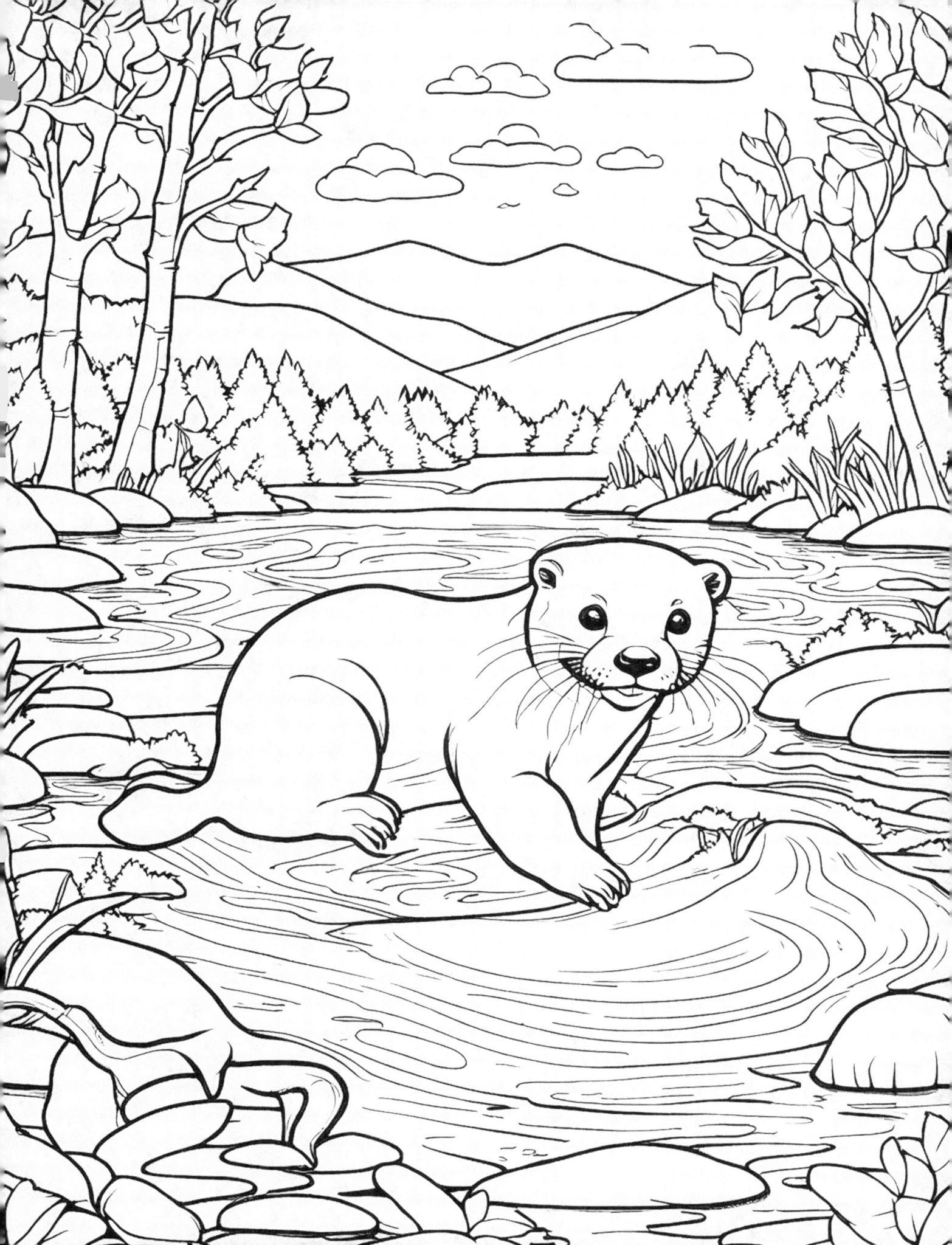